BORING — NEVER!

The Author

BORING —
NEVER!

by

MARGARET E. POPHAM C.B.E.

JOHNSON
———
LONDON

First published 1968

85307 006 7

SET IN 11/12 BASKERVILLE AND PRINTED AND MADE IN GREAT BRITAIN
BY MORRISON AND GIBB LTD., LONDON AND EDINBURGH, FOR JOHNSON
PUBLICATIONS LTD., 11/14 STANHOPE MEWS WEST, LONDON, S.W.7

CONTENTS

∞∞∞

AS OTHERS SEE US   203

At the publishers' suggestion and on representations made during the compilation of this book, the author has agreed to the insertion of the following appreciations:

HER YEARS AT WESTONBIRT by Joy Burden
APPRECIATIONS FROM CHELTENHAM

LIST OF ILLUSTRATIONS

CHAPTER ONE

MY EARLY YEARS

∞∞∞

I HARDLY know where to start. When I retired, a number of people urged me to write my autobiography and I resisted strenuously, and successfully, all such pressures. Now, fourteen years later, having at last yielded, I find myself in the position of having destroyed all my papers and thus removed the support of so many memories that I am at a loss.

So, in the manner of others who have faced this same problem of making a beginning, I shall start with a little about my family and my home background. Indeed, my start in the world of teaching began with my family's close association with this profession in the generations before me; and by the time I had reached the age of five my mind was firmly made up that my one desire was to teach—a resolve which remained unchanged and came to happy fulfilment.

I was born in September 1894 at Woking, where my father was curate at Christ Church. I am told that I spent my first birthday sitting under a table, apparently trying to scratch the face of another little girl who was then two years old. This little girl—from whom I was hastily parted that day—was Nesta Sawyer. She was the daughter of friends of the family and grew up into a gay and splendid woman.

I was evidently an aggressive baby, but I always loved dolls—maybe that could have been the germ of the schoolmarm stirring in me—and when very young I craved for those ungainly wooden dolls which in those days could be had for a penny. Sometimes when my beloved godmother, Aunt Clara, bought one for me, my exultation was unbounded. In addition to my school of dolls there were the tiny matchboxes which Mr. Sawyer used to give me. These were appropriate in size to the stature of my wooden pupils and I used to adapt them—not without that elastic stretch of imagination which is one of the bonuses of childhood—to fabricate all sorts and conditions of things.

It is quite remarkable the number of members of my family whose lives were connected with teaching. The Pophams were in Hampshire even before the Conquest, as is evidenced in the old castle gateway of Winchester, where one appears in the list of Knights of the Shire above King Arthur's Round Table. About three hundred years ago some of the family went over to Cork. My grandfather was brought up there but, after they had been burnt out for being Protestants, he migrated to Ulster and later, being a medical man, came over and set up practice first in Nottingham, and then in London, where he was when, as a child, I knew him. My mother's father was Canon Elliott, a Canon at Windsor: he was a scholar and one of the co-translators of the Revised Version of the Old Testament. He married Mary Rose Babington, first cousin of Thomas Babington Macaulay, with whom she was brought up. They had thirteen children, and I shall have more to say later about my grandmother and those of my aunts and uncles who played a part in my life. In spite of having so many uncles and aunts, I only had seven cousins on that side of the family, and two on the other side, who were the sons of my father's only brother.

One of my Elliott uncles was on the Bristol Senate and was a school inspector. Two others were parsons and a fourth had a preparatory school. One of my aunts lived with this brother, so she also clearly had an interest in education herself. Aunt Clara, who lived with my grandmother, was a tireless and devoted Sunday School teacher: so that, right up to the time of her death at the age of fifty-two, by which time I had left the university, she had a great influence over me.

Aunt Florence, the eldest of my aunts, lived in Stepney where she devoted her life to teaching and training vanboys. She did this, mainly, by telling stories. Once, when I went to see her, I found her seated in a hall, surrounded by a company of the roughest looking vanboys and men, talking to them. Except for my aunt's quiet and pleasant voice, the silence was absolute. She was small and plain and had not the presence to command interest until she started to talk, but, when she did so, her goodness and love of all people was so obvious that it compelled the attention of her audience—and their sympathetic response.

I have few remembrances of Woking except, of course, that it was far more of a country town than it is today, but I have many fragrant memories of the pine woods nearby. My greatest excitement was to go for a walk with my father, whom I adored, and many and delightful were the treasures of nature he revealed to me. I have ever been grateful to him for teaching me how rich are the rewards to those who keep their eyes open.

On one important occasion, however, we did not see so much.

We had walked across the fields which lay between our house and the railway to watch a train go by. It was a very special train—in it rode the 'great Queen'—Queen Victoria. In order that I might see her, my father lifted me on to his shoulder. But, alas! All I saw, as the train went over the railway bridge was the top of her bonnet. Yet this attempt to see the Queen is still vivid in my memory, for I then had my first idea of patriotism and of being a part of history.

We left Woking when I was four, as my father became Rector of Shoeburyness. Our house there had a huge garden, including an orchard, a flower garden and a kitchen garden and large lawns set out for croquet. This was a joy to my parents as they were both very fond of gardening and, although it entailed, as all gardens do, much exacting labour, they also found time to go in for bee-keeping and poultry. The latter was my mother's hobby.

I was somewhat indifferent to the garden; but the dogs were my unbounded love of those days. My dolls were my vocation—

the dogs my love. Of these—we had three—my deepest love was Nero. He was a black retriever with beautiful, loving brown eyes. He was highly intelligent, but he could play the silly when the occasion demanded and accompanied me wherever I went —a splendid guide, guardian and friend. Daily he went round the orchard carrying a basket which my mother filled with eggs —eggs from hens who had plenty of space to move about and were not cooped up in tiny cages as they so often are now. Then there was an Irish terrier and a Scotty. The latter attended church every time the bells rang! Normally he sat in the vestry, but when we had a curate who preached longer than usual, he solemnly walked down the chancel and sat, head on one side, gazing at him. This nice Mr. Squire said it was the best training he ever had and that never again would he preach too long anywhere.

Just in front of the house lay a common—beyond that, the sea. It was a lovely environment for a child, but I did not have the freedom of a child of today fully to enjoy it. I had a nurse and, looking back in retrospect, I consider that the modern child is a great deal luckier than we were in those days. If children nowadays have nannies at all, it is for a far shorter time. The result is that they listen to adult conversation much earlier and thus acquire a foundation of worldly knowledge. I was closely shepherded by Nanny wherever I went and was not even allowed into the kitchen to talk to the other servants, such as the cook, from whom also I might have learned much. Then I wanted to learn to cook, but now, with no training behind me, I have perforce to do it and I fear that it is to me a joyless burden.

Whatever I might have learned from them, or from the talk of my parents and their friends, would without a shadow of doubt immediately have been passed on to my dolls. I always wanted to teach my dolls everything I knew. It was my daily occupation to wash them and dress them and lecture them. Above all, they were forever having school. I loved passing on knowledge. The idea that all knowledge is given us so that we may give it to others was germinating in me, doubtless as a result of my share of the family inheritance. Certainly, my love of teaching was already quickening in those far-off days.

When I was four and a half years old, my sister was born. I had always adored dogs and dolls, and I know I should have been thrilled if my parents had told me in the right manner that she was coming. Unfortunately for me, and for some years for my sister, the event was pitched at me without warning and found me unprepared. Instead of being thrilled and delighted, I was frightened and hurt. The stupidity of a housemaid exacerbated the wound.

I had no idea why my mother was in bed.

'Why? Why? Why?' I wondered. No one had the sense to tell me and so allay my disquietude.

Finally, when the housemaid was taking me up to see my mother, she announced:

'Now your mother has a new baby, and she won't love you any more.'

What a thing to say to a child! I was shattered!

I was at an inarticulate age and could not frame the right questions in order to discover how wrong and wicked she was. It is not surprising that, from that moment, I disliked my sister intensely. My relationship with my father was unaffected, but I had a much diminished trust in my mother. For years I never outgrew this feeling. It lasted until I was almost grown up, despite my sister's invariable kindness and sweet temper. One could not have wished for a more gentle and understanding person.

My mother was a beautiful woman and my sister took after her, while also showing a strong likeness to my father. She was pretty, fair-haired with a beautiful complexion; while I, as a child, was podgy with masses of tangled hair. Oh, the brushing that went on! I was a messy child and I do not suppose my demon of jealousy added to my attraction when I was with her. For I have to confess that I was often bad-tempered when, as a baby, she disturbed my dolls' houses and other appurtenances.

However, she always took it in good part and, in the future, when we grew up, we were to become fast friends.

Loveday Home, my sister was christened, these being two Popham family names. After going to a Domestic Science School, she did what my mother always wanted me to do and stayed as a good daughter at home. When my father retired and moved to Ditchling in Sussex, he sensibly bought a house in her name and there she still is, living as a widow after marrying a man whom she had known for twenty-five years and who was twenty years older than she was. We are still excellent friends.

Not all stories of youthful jealousy between members of a family end on so happy a note: and such an experience as mine was unnecessary. The young today are so much luckier in being given the proper information: it is one of the things that we owe to the closer rapport between parents and children and the more intimate attitude towards the young that is one of the good features of the post-war years.

In our days at Shoeburyness I had little companionship. My only friends were Rex Hillier, the schoolmaster's son, and the gardener's son, but they were nice lads and I was happy in their friendship. Life was mostly confined to the garden and the sea. We were so much in the country that the busy garrison town—though not a busy place by today's standards—with all its activity seemed something removed from the quiet tenor of our country life. I was taken there just occasionally. Once, I remember, I was taken to see a pantomime at the garrison, to the pleasure of which was added the excitement of going there in the one village cab.

Then, on one great occasion, my father took me to London to stay with my Popham grandfather. He lived in Kensington Gardens Square and I was terrified of the house which, to me, seemed so high and forbidding, but my fears dissolved before the kindness of the maid, Sarah, who made my visit pleasant by giving me a nightlight to go to bed with. One of the landmarks of that visit was the opening of Whiteley's 'Universal' Stores, which ceremony we attended. Then there was my grandfather's balcony, on which there was a huge cage, loud with the twitter of many brightly coloured birds. What delighted me was that the cage was so big that the birds could fly freely about it.

Even life in a rectory was very different in those days. For we were able to have a cook, a housemaid, a nurse and a gardener, as were the other parsons whom we knew. As it has turned out, this was not particularly good from an educational point of view, for I never learned to do anything practical, other than sewing. Here, fortunately, I was able to acquire some proficiency, as, by the time I had collected all my dolls, both large and small, I wanted to dress them and my mother, who was a good sempstress, taught me. At Shoeburyness, when Aunt Clara and other visitors came to stay, they usually came for a month and arrived with a round-topped trunk in considerable state in the one available cab from the station. There was in those days no going away merely for the weekend. Children's clothes were also different—bodices, flannel petticoats with beautifully scalloped bottoms done by mother, stiffly starched and embroidered white petticoats—how uncomfortable and bulky they were. Then we had pinafores to wear in the mornings—all such a bore. Large velour hats for winter and Leghorn ones for summer. Today's children don't know how lucky they are to be free of all this!

Money was never mentioned: that would have been vulgar. Later on, when we had moved to Lee and I was at school I remember mentioning at lunch that one of my friends was very rich and how much pocket-money she had. I was told that to talk of money at a meal was not done by educated people. How life has changed! I also remember at Lee our starting off for a summer holiday in Derbyshire where my father had taken a locum tenens. We each had a trunk and mother had a hat-box all of which went on to the roof of a big cab. Then father's bicycle and mine had to be tied on. Looking back, I can see what a funny spectacle it was and why the people opposite came out to see us.

I was never really taught anything while I was little, not even to read. I had a book of the 'Cat: C-A-T' kind, but no proper teaching until I was about nine or ten years old. At this stage, Mr. Hillier, headmaster of the village school, started to come for an hour on Saturday mornings, during which time he taught me to write from a copybook and to do brushwork. This latter consisted of making leaves and flowers with a single stroke of the brush, rather as did the Zen Buddhist artists of China. This method of introduction to painting and drawing was very much favoured in those Edwardian days. However, I have to confess that at both these occupations I was extremely untidy and dirty.

Later on, I had a governess, but I never remember any lessons from her! It seems as if I spent most of my time with my dolls, teaching them before I started learning anything myself!

This lack of early training in reading has been a disadvantage to me all my life. For, as a result, I read much more slowly than most people do and in these circumstances it is far more difficult to grasp the sense of an entire book or document—one tends to forget the beginning of it before one has ploughed through to the end! However, once I learned to read, I did everything I could to make up for lost time and I waded steadily through Walter Scott, Charles Dickens, Charlotte Brontë, Jane Austen and other nineteenth-century writers: likewise the adventure stories in *Chums* or any other magazine I could get hold of.

On Sundays throughout my childhood my mother used to read books to us of the kind specially selected for Sunday reading, such as *A Peep Behind the Scenes*, *Ministering Children* and *Wide, Wide World*. In this latter I still recollect a depressing child who wept all the time, which has never been my own idea of what childhood should be.

I owe a great deal of my early education to the frequent visits I made to my grandmother, both before I went to school and during holidays later on. I remember going to her in the summer when I was twelve. She lived at St. Leonard's and, as I have said, my Aunt Clara with her. The whole life there was a joy, for my aunt would take me to the beach with its fascinating rocks and shells, or she would take me for walks and to visit in her 'District', and tell me about the children in her Sunday School. As I grew older I was thrilled to get to know the Streatfeild family, who were distant cousins. I used to admire them in the days when we went to Hastings Castle, and I have kept up with Noel and admire her even now. Then, too, Walter Besant lived opposite my grandmother and I used to see his daughter, and I was thrilled to have glimpses of him, for I had read *All Sorts and Conditions of Men* which interested me, although I do not remember any other of his books. Apart from the delightful parties we attended and the interest of getting to know people, I learned so much from my grandmother herself. One of those lucky people with photographic memory, she was an avid reader and could in no time assimilate a book and retell the whole contents. Equally, she could remember books which she had read years before. I remember once when I was twelve she talked of Pusey and was so horrified at my not having heard of him that she made me read his life. Then I was given the life of Wilberforce, and so gradually became deeply interested in the whole Tractarian Movement. This led me during one holiday to read the *Apologia* of Newman with further interesting talks with Granny, who told me so much about his life. Indeed years later, when doing the Cambridge Teachers' Diploma, I had to study his *Idea of a University* and I was surprised to realise how much of it I had learnt unconsciously from my grandmother. Born at the time of Queen Victoria's Coronation, she had known so many of the people of the nineteenth century. She was, when I knew her, an old lady in a lace cap, with a brilliant mind which had never dimmed. She died two days before her ninety-fourth birthday, having walked that day down the hill to Hastings to vote in an election and back again.

That night, instead of ringing the bell punctually at 10 p.m. to summon the servants to prayers, to my aunt's amazement she continued knitting a shawl for an old woman in the district. When Aunt Clara asked if she realised the time, she said she must finish the shawl. This she did, then rang the bell and after prayers went to bed and died in her sleep. What a glorious way to die! I only wish all old people could have the same good fortune. I think we should all be allowed to live as long as we are happy and interested, but surely it is wrong for doctors to prolong the life—which is not real life—of those who become incapacitated or suffer and long to pass on.

In 1906, when I was twelve, father moved to Holy Trinity, Lee, S.E., and I began to attend Blackheath High School. Unhappily, illness kept me away for most of the first two years. But I adored the school and never missed a day except when I was forced to. There was one heartbreaking period when I was kept away for a long time with quinsy, which developed into pleurisy and then pneumonia. In the course of this I was unconscious and delirious for days; I remember that I regained consciousness while the doctor was talking to Mother.

'Yes! The worst is past,' I heard him say. 'She should be all right.'

I remember saying inwardly:

'Jesus, do You want me to teach? If so, I will live! If not, let me die—please!'

This may seem a curious attitude for a child, but it does show, I think, how powerful even in those days must have been my urge to teach. It was a true vocation.

Although my mother was immensely good to me whilst I was ill and brought me books to read and transfers to stick into a scrapbook, which kept me amused, my only desire was to get back to school. Miss Gadesden was headmistress then and what a wonderful headmistress she was. What character! What personality! Still, today, the sound of heels clicking across a parquet floor brings back memories of her clicking across the Big Hall and the old deep affection I had for her surges up anew. And all the rest of the staff! Never can I be grateful enough to them. There was Miss Crabbé—a genius at making geography interesting; Miss Baldwin, so brilliant at unravelling the mysteries of mathematics, and, in later days, Miss Ethel Winnington Ingram, niece of the Bishop of London, who inspired in me a true appreciation and love of English poetry. Like myself, she came from a family of parsons and teachers. Her sister, Miss Maude Winnington Ingram, was on the staff of Cheltenham when I went there in 1937: she had meant to retire that year, but I persuaded her to stay on. Finally there was Miss Winifred Fisher to whom I owe my undying love of history; and thanks to whose advice I eventually went to Westfield College, London University. I can truly say that Blackheath gave me unimpaired joy and happiness—and much more beyond that.

At the start I was taken to school by Miss Morris, my governess, and at the time I revolted stubbornly against this. I longed to be like the others who cycled to school. Even when I walked on my own, I had to follow the school rule and take a note to the headmistress, signed by my parents, naming the girls with whom I was permitted to walk to school. I had a great many friends then, especially the Moss twins whom I used to meet as we went the same way. Then there were Margaret Green and Marjorie Cadman, the latter of whom kept up with me until her untimely death in her forties. Then, too, there was the Dyson family whose father was Astronomer Royal. How I used to enjoy going to Greenwich, for the park was always lovely and it was a great day when Sir Frank Watson Dyson took us into the Observatory to see the huge telescopes. The river too was a great attraction at Greenwich. On Saturday with other friends I used sometimes to go on a barge trip to Kew and back. This was a fascinating experience and in those days it cost us only 6*d* each. It was a great thrill to see the docks along the bank which, in my thoughts, I would associate with my father's stories of his days at Deptford before I was born, when he was curate there.

Blackheath, too, had its attractions with its many Regency and Georgian residential houses and the round pond. There were in those days no cars to spoil the peace and charm. Occasionally too we made expeditions to study botany in the ponds at Hayes and to enjoy the open country outside Bromley and Eltham. We in our day had to walk and bicycle everywhere and were not pampered by being taken in state-provided buses as are the children of today.

But at least foolish snobbery is out these days and boys and girls are left to make their own friends. Admittedly they often make mistakes to start with and I have known girls make great friends with other girls with whom they have fundamentally little in common. But then they broaden out and find other friends whose interests and background they share. I well remember, years later, a parent coming to me to say she did not like a certain friend her daughter had chosen. I suggested that she invite the other girl to spend a few days of her holidays at their home. Under these circumstances and against the background of an intellectual and cultured home, the two girls realised for themselves that a close friendship was not likely to continue.

At this age my enthusiasm for reading truly ran riot. I was given a penny a day for biscuits and milk, but I used to spend it on little pink books—the notorious 'penny novelettes' of Victorian days—which were an adventure into a different type of reading from that to which I had been accustomed. At that age they seemed much more exciting to me and there must have been some reference in them which aroused my curiosity, for I remember one day asking my mother how babies were born.

'Well, dear, I really don't know,' she replied. 'God starts it and the doctor does the rest.'

This was the entire extent of sex knowledge vouchsafed to me. In any case, we just never talked about sex at school—it was never in our minds. We did have violent arguments about history; we were Roundheads or Cavaliers, Protestants or Catholics, according to what period we were reading and at the same time characters in historical novels connected with any such period.

Then, towards the end of my schooldays, the Suffragette Movement burst in on us. I learnt all about this from my friend, Margaret Green, whose home was one in which all such matters were discussed continually in contrast to my own—in which my mother thought that all such fuss was unnecessary. At school Votes for Women was our principal topic. Margaret Green was a very potent influence in broadening my mind in those days. Being a very late developer, a trait I inherited from my mother's family, I was more immature in personality development than other girls all the way through school, and I owe much to my many friendships, especially that with Margaret.

As my schooldays drew to a close, I began to dream about going on to university, but it was always quite clear to me that my mother was determined that I should not go. She wanted me to be a 'good daughter' at home, and then to marry. I meant to teach. It was not until two terms before I was due to leave that Miss Gadesden at length persuaded my family that I should go.

Before going to university, however, there were stiles to be crossed. I had to matriculate. For this I had to learn Latin, as I had never been allowed to study that language. This meant special coaching for my last two terms at school. This became both an excitement and an anxiety to me, for, although I was always near or at the top of my class, it was due to hard work and enthusiasm, for I lacked the grounding of those who had gone to school early. I came to love Latin, but, having learned it in six months, I promptly forgot it during the next five for, except where people are concerned, I have a very bad memory. I did not keep it up, as I did not realise I would need it at university. Fortunately, however, I got through my exam and I was ready for the next move forward towards my ambition to become a qualified teacher.

Before I close this chapter of my early life and school days, there are two events which merit inclusion. One because I was an eye-witness to an historic event—and anything involving history has ever been important to me, and the other because it underlines, once more, how first and foremost my desire to learn so that I might teach, has ever been my Lode Star.

The first event was a royal one, though sad. It was the

funeral of King Edward VII. My parents took me to Windsor Castle for this, and from the Round Tower we saw the train go by which carried the coffin containing the body of the dead monarch to burial. I remember that it was draped in purple and the sun shone on it and added brilliance to the scene.

The second event, though different, was equally unforgettable. Together with two other parsons' daughters, without my parents' knowledge, I went off to the Mile End Road, of which I had heard all sorts of lurid tales. There we ate baked potatoes off barrows and subsequently got into great trouble for pawning our coats in order to raise enough money for our homeward journey. Our parents reported us to Miss Gadesden who dealt with us all with her usual wisdom and understanding. In my case, she said that if I did such a thing again, I would have to *miss school for a day*. Such a threat was enough to curb my straying tendencies.

I left school finally in 1914, and shortly before I was due to leave my parents moved to Tatsfield Rectory in Surrey. As a consequence I spent the last few weeks of school with my friend, Constance Raymond's family, and for the first time felt really free. At last, it seemed, I had the chance to grow up. I was very lucky at this stage to be moving to the life of Westfield College.

I have told the story of my childhood and hardly mentioned my father. My father always meant very much to me. Indeed he was loved and respected by all who knew him. He was immensely practical and would help villagers in any trouble with gates or doors or whatever it might be. He visited everyone in the parish and they would unburden themselves to him completely. I remember one day when I was about six years old, I was with him when a parishioner stopped him; and at lunch later I said to my mother, 'Oh, we met Mrs. so-and-so, and she said . . .' My father explained then that what one overheard one should never repeat, and the difference between friends and family at home and those who talked to him as The Rector. How useful this was all through life!

Wherever he might be, father's practical ability enabled him to reduce to a mere song the vast sums that the 'dilapidations' would have cost. I remember, too, at Shoeburyness how he got many keen people to help build a village hall and how he worked with the men.

Later—I suppose about 1910 or so, when at Holy Trinity, Lee, he bought an old Cadillac for £5 and, doing the work himself, made it quite efficient. How well I can even now picture him and my mother, who was wrapped up in a 'dust-coat' and had her hat tied on with a huge veil, sitting high up in this noisy vehicle and travelling at about five miles an hour. Eventually he sold that car for £25!

Father's sincerity and simplicity drew everyone to him. When he went to Lee the church was practically empty, and when he left it was full. In spite of the infinitesimal stipend, he at once abolished pew rents, for, said he, the House of God is open to all.

Even after he retired, people would walk long distances to hear him preach in the tiny church at Clayton where for long he officiated. What drew people everywhere was that really he didn't preach in the normal sense of the word, but quite simply in five to seven minutes said what he believed. Also it was obvious that he lived it too. His life was based on the New Testament and the Communion Service. This latter he took beautifully—helped, when he happened to be staying near, by Archbishop Temple.

Both clever and simple people loved him, as did all dogs. I often see in my mind's eye a picture of Boris, his old English sheepdog, with his grey and white curly hair, following him solemnly up and down the lawn at Tatsfield whilst he did the mowing.

CHAPTER TWO

WESTFIELD COLLEGE

∽∽∽

I was fortunate from the first day that I went to Westfield. I was still completely unsophisticated and, in those days, painfully shy. But on the doorstep I fell in with Nora Almond who took me under her wing and has remained a firm friend ever since. Nora, a former student of Westfield, was then on the Classics staff.

In those days Westfield was a small self-contained women's College, but an integral part, as it is now, of the University of London. It was founded in 1882 thanks to the inspiration of Miss Constance Maynard and the generosity of Miss Dudin Brown who donated the sum of £10,000 towards its establishment. Miss Maynard was the first Principal—though she was then called 'the Mistress'. Miss Maynard had come down from Girton with a passionate desire to found in London a college on a Christian basis. That is how Westfield came into being. After thirty-one years of devoted service, during which the College developed and flourished greatly, she retired in 1913 and her place was taken by Miss Agnes de Sélincourt.

How can I convey exactly what Westfield has meant to me? On our arrival Miss de Sélincourt assembled all the Freshers in the homely atmosphere of her own private room, where she talked of the privilege of being a student in Westfield, and told us of the past and emphasised its religious foundation. From that first evening Westfield was another home to me. I have loved it ever since. In these days of great educational development, I am proud to have been until quite recently a member of its Council.

24

Westfield College

Even in those days Westfield was a spacious place. The building had all the pleasant proportions of late nineteenth-century architecture: and every student had her own inter-communicating bedroom and sitting-room. The gardens were a real joy, as was its situation on the heights of Hampstead. It was good to be able to walk so easily with friends across Hampstead Heath and look from our vantage point right across to Hendon. Old Hampstead, too, had its charms, many of which are still preserved today.

In those days we could bicycle everywhere unhindered by today's bane of the ubiquitous motor car, whether to University College or to King's for special lectures, or to see plays from the gallery of the Old Vic, and at times even to slip down in the evenings to help the war workers in the crypt of St. Martin's-in-the-Fields, where Dick Sheppard was then the vicar. On Sundays, since the nearby church was ultra-evangelical and, to our lively young minds, somewhat dull, one or two of us would go down to listen to that broad-minded and interesting preacher Percy Dearmer, at his church on Primrose Hill. He attracted us by his magnetic personality and the beauty of his services. Also, to my mind rightly, he laid far less emphasis on sermons and far more on the Communion Service. With this I have been in agreement all my life and it was a bone of contention as far as I was concerned with the ultra-evangelicals in Canada. My own problem has always been that, being tone deaf and quite unmusical, I never worshipped as wholeheartedly in a Choral Communion as in the simple service. Therefore, I find myself now going either at 8 a.m. or 12 noon to Communion, rather than to any other Service. The friend who first led me to Percy Dearmer's services was an old Paulina, Katherine Wakefield. As she was also reading Classics we came naturally to be friends.

Miss de Sélincourt was a most striking personality in addition to her outstanding scholarship. She had dark hair and dark eyes, which seemed to flash when she was moved or was angry. She dressed beautifully, had immense poise and endless charm. She would receive students in a tasteful and softly lighted room. I suppose, having endured the glare and garish glitter of India, she preferred a kindly and subdued light. She detested a harsh light. I shall never forget how she talked to us that evening on my first entry.

It was at Westfield, under the wise and kindly guidance of Miss de Sélincourt, that I began to grow up—to feel free and to realise that, at last, I was seriously preparing for the career which had been my dream since childhood. I have often wondered what she thought of me in those early days, for, judging by the comments of my contemporaries, I must have been an untidy and erratic student. On the credit side was my unflagging enthusiasm and happiness in hard work. I loved the college—I never asked for an exeat, simply because I could not bear to be absent from it—even for a night.

Being a small community, we saw a good deal of our lecturers. Often we went to their rooms for cocoa in the evenings and thus got to know them well and were able to discuss all kinds of subjects. On Sundays, the Principal continued to hold meetings which had been begun by Miss Maynard and which were called 'Function'. Students assembled in the large and comfortable common-room, somewhere about six o'clock, and she would talk to us. Generally she spoke on some religious subject and sometimes she told us of her work in India. Occasionally an outside speaker was invited to give a talk and these talks were invariably fascinating and provocative of thought and of discussion. It was undoubtedly on account of Miss de Sélincourt and Dr. McDougall and because so many Westfield students went out to India and other parts of the world as missionaries, that we heard so much about India in particular. I longed to go there throughout my life, and when in retirement I went to stay with Indian friends it brought back many memories of Westfield days.

On one evening each week Dr. McDougall welcomed anyone who might be interested to her room for what she called 'Myths'. She told us about the Greek legends, their origin and meaning and how they had influenced modern philosophy and creative thinking. These talks were of unfailing interest, for Dr. McDougall had a great depth of scholarship and was a person of vision. My first academic encounter with her was painfully humiliating. During my first year, I had to work for my Intermediate B.A., and the first lecture in Latin to which I went nearly proved disastrous. For reasons which I have already explained, my Latin would have disgraced a fourth former. Unfortunately during the lecture Dr. McDougall asked me to translate one of Horace's Odes. If only, at that moment, I could have vanished into thin air! I had to confess that I was incapable of doing any such thing, whereupon she said I would have to leave the class.

Typically she had afterthoughts. During the afternoon, she came to my room and told me that she had not realised the cursory nature of my experience in this language. In view of this she said that, of course, I could return to her lectures. Such generosity of spirit was typical of her. She was shortly afterwards to leave Westfield to become Principal of Madras Christian College.

Of all the subjects I was taking the one I still enjoyed most was History and, under the inspiring teaching of Miss Sergeant —later Mrs. Wellington—I became enthralled and turned my mind determinedly towards specialising in it. The History School, of which Dr. Skeel was the Senior Professor, played an important part in Westfield. Miss Skeel was an outstanding human being and scholar, and gave much inspiration not only to her own students, but also to all of us who came into contact with her. She, too, has played an important part in the development of the college. She lived simply in a small house with a maid right up to the last: but she inherited money from a millionaire brother and her bequests to the college provided much towards its new buildings. Looking back on Westfield, what strikes me most is the number of people like Miss Skeel who were really dedicated to the college and prepared to serve it to the n'th degree. This must I think be the reason why so many of its students of all generations are imbued with real affection for it.

However, under Miss Parker and Nora Almond, I now got on fast with Latin, and, at the end of the year, the latter persuaded me to read Classics. I was all the more ready to do this, for I eagerly wanted to begin Greek. Academically this was unwise, but I have no regrets, for I always loved it and, without it, would never have been introduced to Plato, Aristotle and Pinder who became and have since stayed my favourite authors. Also, as it turned out, it was invaluable to have studied a variety of subjects when, as Head of schools, I had to listen to classes and judge methods of teaching. I am convinced that, for any position of leadership and command, the broadening and liberalisation of the mind through a Classical education is the soundest foundation. Also, although I was never really a scholar, it helped me to inspire many to go much further than I myself had gone.

Being under Miss Parker—affectionately known as 'Pook'—was a delightful experience. I never missed a lecture and enjoyed each one to the full. Another pleasurable advantage was that she used to take the Classics students for reading parties in the vacation. I remember one glorious day in Surrey when we cycled from Dorking to Shere, where we had a delightful time reading and blackberrying. On such excursions we always used to bicycle and I retain a vivid picture of Pook, a miniscule figure in navy coat and skirt and straw hat perched precariously on top of a head of wispy hair, whose combinations remorselessly insisted on gradually descending down and down her legs over her stockings. She herself was quite unconscious of such things!

At that time I was reading much of Dostoievsky and she would often talk to us about his novels, commenting on his philosophy and then going on to talk of Plato, Aristotle and other Greek thinkers. Talking or lecturing, it made no difference; she was always fascinating. Her Plato lectures were outstanding and left a deeper impression on me than anything

28

else I have learnt anywhere. Even lectures on grammar were interesting, but at times we teased her. I remember one lecture when she was urging us to study Robey's grammar more thoroughly, a student said, 'George Robey, Miss Parker?' Looking puzzled, she said, 'I don't know his Christian name,' and had no idea why we all smiled.

After I left, I still went several times to France and Italy with Pook and Nora, and we always kept in touch. When I was at Westonbirt Miss Parker had retired to live near Bristol, and it was a joy to visit her in her old age and find her still full of humour and in touch with her Westfield students.

Equally inspiring as a lecturer was Miss Alford; although the first time I went to one of her lectures I was too absorbed in watching her and fascinated by her as a person to profit much from it. She was a tall, dignified person, with straight hair drawn tightly back into a bun. What distracted me was the way she periodically pulled up her voluminous black skirt to extract, from a deep pocket in an equally voluminous bright green underskirt, a vast white handkerchief.

I marvelled at the profundity of her knowledge. It seemed to me remarkable that anyone could devote a two-hour lecture, without interest flagging for one moment, to a single sentence of Cicero. I am sure it was mainly from her that I first began to understand the meaning of true scholarship. With all this she remained quite oblivious of the quality of her mind and, being completely unassuming, I doubt if she ever suspected the extent of the outer darkness of people like myself.

Once when I asked: 'Will you please explain something to me?' she replied: 'Willingly! But I cannot promise to elucidate the recondite.' From so dedicated a scholar, I am confident we gained a new concept of the sanctity of work and learning and appreciation of the genuine humility which nearly always accompanies great minds such as hers.

As I remember, it must have been in the summer of 1915 that I went with Nora Almond and her mother up to Scotland. After staying a while in Aberdeen, where one of her brothers was in the Seaforth Highlanders (he was later to be killed in the Battle of the Somme in 1916) we went to visit the foothills of the Cairngorms.

There we met an exceptional old lady—indeed, we stayed for a week with her in her Highland cottage. And what a cottage! It was situated deep in the woods.

Our landlady was a fitting denizen of such an enchanted spot. She was the dearest of people and cozened and cosseted us in all manner of kindly ways. She baked glorious scones for our tea—eaten with enormous fresh eggs with 'blaeberry' jam to follow. With an excellent dinner of venison she served a jelly of the same berry. She was a quaint but dignified person and, as is not uncommon in those parts, a staunch Roman Catholic. She deplored the war and insisted that: 'There wouldn'a ha' been one ony way, had a'body stuck to the true Church and not permeeted yon bit mannie Knox, wi' a' his horde o' die'ls, tae introduce his pisen into Britain.' What John Knox's Calvinistic missions had to do with German ambitions of aggrandisement, I leave it to my readers to work out. On Sunday a dog-cart came to take her to Mass. We absolutely revelled in her and marvelled, when, after the first night, she asked us if 'half a croon' would be too much to ask for supper, bed and breakfast!

Time there passed all too quickly. We were so happy. I was utterly content, relaxed in the kind hospitality of our 'dear old lady', quietly to pursue my studies of Greek and Latin and to wander the hillsides gathering sphagnum moss which we sent for dressings to hospitals.

Whilst the Almonds stayed on in Aberdeen I went south to stay with Olga Masaryk during part of the vacation. Olga was the younger daughter of Professor Masaryk and we had become friends at Westfield. The Masaryks lived at Hampstead and my train back to Euston was terribly late. When I arrived, all London was enveloped in the inky darkness of the black-out. I could find no conveyance of any sort, size or condition, neither taxi nor tram, so there was nothing for it but shank's mare.

London held no fears for me nor had I any fears—it was comparatively safe in those days. But how I found my way through all the noisome and sinister streets in the purlieus of Camden Town, to this day I could not say! I know I lost my way and went back on my tracks several times, but at last I found myself in Finchley Road. I knew my way from there but it was two in the morning when eventually, rather fearful and ashamed, I rang the bell.

I need not have worried. Olga had said she would expect me at any time and was not upset. When I rang the bell, however, the burglar alarm went off and the white-bearded professor called out to know what had happened. Worse still, it went off again when I opened my bedroom window. Olga called to him, 'It's all right! It's only Pop wanting some air!' and he exclaimed, 'Air! Who can want air at night?'

Olga and I had much in common and, though an irreproachable host, the professor was wrapped up in his work and we saw little of him. All the world knows of the stature of that great man and I feel it would be presumptuous of me to try to add anything to the story of one who has become one of the heroes of history. Personally I was impressed by his immense dignity, though, on my first visit, I found him a shade awe-inspiring. When at a later date I visited the Masaryks in their charming home in Bistryka, outside Prague, he could not have been more natural. Periodically Olga and I continued to keep in touch and I have always had a deep sympathy for that tragic family. Once we met somewhere in Europe—I think in Switzerland. I was at Westonbirt when she invited me to Czechoslovakia. With Maud Kidney, of whom I speak later, I went out by car across Germany—it must have been the summer of 1933—which I hated. I am so glad that I saw Olga in her home before the Second World War overwhelmed their country. I admired the way all the family unhesitatingly spoke English, German, French or Czech according to whom they were speaking. Following this visit I was not to see Olga again until after the war when she was in London, sad and suffering from the tragic

31

death of her brother, Jan, and the loss of her beloved son in the war. This was before she left to join her sister in the U.S.A.

In the summer of 1917, a sad shadow was cast over us all. Miss Parker and Nora had all our group of Classic students on a reading party at Haslemere. Mrs. Gurney had lent us two cottages on the hillside behind her house where we lived amongst gorse and heather. From here the Devil's Punchbowl was a sight worth seeing, especially at sunset when it lit up the gold and purple. It was an ideal spot for a reading party that September. Then we heard of the tragic death of Miss de Sélincourt as the result of a bicycling accident. It came as a terrible shock as we realised what a tremendous loss her death would mean to the college.

When we all went up for the autumn term Miss Richardson, the Vice-Principal, had been appointed Acting Principal. She was a brilliant Classical scholar, tall and handsome and in every way a commanding personality. She had a splendid head of white hair which, I remember, looked quite magnificent above the stately dress of red velvet which she wore in the evenings. She could not be made Principal as she was not a member of the Church of England: she was a Quaker and her religion was profoundly and sincerely a reality to her. She lectured inspiringly in a deep, attractive voice, and her sessions on Greek philosophy were an inspiration. I always went in awe of her, but very much admired her. She was a dedicated scholar and it was said that she was so preoccupied with intellectual thoughts that, once, she went out with the hearth brush in her hand instead of her umbrella. I hold no brief for the truth of this!

More to the point is the immense circle of friends whom she had and whom she brought into contact with Westfield. I do not know whether it was she who persuaded Dr. William Temple, later Bishop of Manchester and Archbishop of York, then of Canterbury, to be Chairman, and afterwards Sir Thomas Inskip, later Lord Caldecote. It was Temple's fascinating divinity lectures on his book *Mens Creatrix*, which was published in 1917, that were inspiring enough to make me conscious, even

1. Westfield College, 1914

2. Tester

now, of his influence. Later I was to know him much better and once we coincided on the Orient Express when he and Mrs. Temple were going to Jerusalem and I, I think, to Athens on my way to Cairo. His visit to Cheltenham I will mention later. I always used to read his books as they came out and his *Readings in St. John's Gospel* were of infinite value whilst I was teaching Scripture and taking Prayers at Cheltenham.

Evelyn Gedge tells me that, after she became Secretary to the Council and Miss Philpotts was Principal, he often, even after retiring from the chair and moving North, used to visit the College.

Evelyn Gedge and I first met when she did some teaching in the College before I went down. Then again we met at the Kent Classical Society meetings when she and A. K. Clarke were in Gravesend and I in Chatham. It must have been in 1921 or 1922 that I went to Venice with Pook and Nora, and there again Evelyn turned up and we all went on to Florence. Ever since, we have kept in touch through Classics, or through our many mutual friends when I was in Canada, and again when I was on the Westfield Council. As I write now, this morning she was breakfasting with me. A deeply spiritual person, a great church woman, now for a long time a 'Village Evangelist', she is as alive and keenly interested in her friends as she was when I first knew her fifty years ago. She radiates vitality and one always feels better for being with her.

Of my contemporaries at Westfield I have always kept in close touch with Irene Curnow (now Marsingal-Thomas) whose daughters later came to Cheltenham. Emily Wolstencroft and I exchange letters every Christmas. Winifred Galbraith turns up at intervals, from China or Africa, from Leeds University or her Sussex home. Lucia MacWorth Young (now Beamish) is one I've seen at times. Her family and my Elliott relations have, I think, some distant connections. She had a brilliant brain and read philosophy and was an outstanding personality. Many others I see at intervals, also many of other generations whom I sent up from all my schools.

Boring—Never!

I could write reams about those happy days spent at Westfield, but, looking back after so many years, memory plays me the knave. But my most worthwhile recollection is, of course, the way in which those two great women, Miss de Sélincourt and Miss Richardson influenced my life. Both, through brilliance and profound religious spirit, exercised a deep and abiding influence over all who came under their direction. Through her Sunday talks Miss de Sélincourt gave us a vision of service, one which each student could realise through her own particular vocation whilst we gained an enormous amount from the example she set.

Prayers, too, were part of the vital spirit which pervaded the College. In my time they were held in the Library and meant much to most of us. I still cherish the copies of *Pilgrim's Progress*, *Holy War* and other books which Miss de Sélincourt gave at the end of each year to those who never missed Prayers.

Not so happy a memory of those days was the anxiety of the war and, even more immediate to me, my own anxiety over my work. I always was an erratic student and my Greek and Latin prose varied from alpha plus to gamma minus. Miss Parker always contended that I should get either a First or a Third. Her worst fears were realised. I got an ignominious Third! At the time I was very downcast, but, looking back over the experience of the years, I do not believe it has made any difference to my career, except that, having done a good deal of work for a Ph.D. by the time I was invited to Canada and having had to abandon this to take up my appointment at Havergal, I knew then that scholarship must in my life be deserted for the sake of teaching.

In those days, we had to take Finals in the autumn. I remember, that summer, spending a weekend with Miss Maynard. She had known my Popham grandmother, who died before I was born, but whom she remembered well. Soon after my arrival, she took me round her garden and, pointing to a rose tree, she said, 'That is dear Miss McDougall,' to a shrub: 'That is Miss Whitby.' She thought so much of her Westfield friends and the plants each had given her. Her heart was still very much in the college she had founded and for which she had done so much. When I told her that I was no scholar she had words to cheer me. She said that I was a very late developer but that, often, late developers did best in the end. I did not see her again until one day, when I was at Westonbirt, she wrote asking me to go and see her in the house she had moved into at Gerrards Cross. Although by then she was a very old lady she was still talking of the College with all her former love and affection.

Before my Finals in 1918, I spent about a month at Westfield and thus came, for a brief period, under Miss Philpotts who had been appointed Principal. I could not, therefore, know a great deal about her, but the painting of her in the College shows her as a person of outstanding attraction. I was lucky enough to be able for a short while to attend her engrossing talks on Iceland and its literature.

So, not without a pain in my heart, my happy days at Westfield came to an end. But it was not a parting. Years later I was appointed to the Council, of which for thirty-one years I was a member, and that to my joy has kept me closely in touch with the College and its progress.

CHAPTER THREE

CHATHAM COUNTY SCHOOL

∞∞

To FILL IN the six weeks between Finals and the Christmas holidays, I went to Leytonstone College to teach Latin and English to the junior boys. I enjoyed these very responsive small boys and found plenty of amusement during these few weeks. It was still the early weeks following the Armistice; the younger masters were not demobilised and I found the older ones rather awe-inspiring. At breakfast they sat at a huge table using only alternate chairs. As no one appeared to wish for a neighbour, I decided that I had better sit in each empty chair in turn. Apart from that, I do not remember anything about the school except that the Headmaster and the Housekeeper were very pleasant. The only annoyance was that the big gates were closed at 10 o'clock—probably the continuation of a war-time measure. I quite enjoyed my experience, and had earned a little money.

Chatham County School, my first real post, gave me in a sense my first real freedom. I went there in January 1919 very happily, for I had already met Miss Wakeman, the Headmistress, when I had been sent by Westfield for an interview. This had its funny side. I cannot remember where it was, except that it was in London. Having arrived in good time and been shown into an empty room, I hung out of the window hoping to see her arrive.

'Is that Miss Popham? If so, I would rather see your face than your legs.' I suddenly heard a voice behind me: Miss Wakeman had entered the room.

36

After that rather embarrassing start, she asked why I had chosen to read Classics and why I had so much loved West-field.

Then suddenly she interjected, 'Do you make howlers?'

'Yes,' I admitted. 'Badly, sometimes.'

'Then you should be able to teach your pupils not to: can you?'

'I don't know,' I said, 'but I will try.'

Then she said, surprisingly: 'You realise that I am offering you the post.'

I certainly had not realised this, but I accepted with alacrity, for I recognised in Miss Wakeman the signs of a great head-mistress.

She was of very small build and had lovely auburn hair. That day, as always, she was immaculately dressed in a well-cut coat and skirt. Her eyes were penetrating and she never missed a thing. The outstanding feature was her firm chin, which showed her character. She was, as one could see, a strong disciplinarian, but she had both charm and sense of humour. I told her at the interview that I could only stay either two terms, or a year and two terms, as I had scholarships to go to the Cambridge Train-ing College. This she accepted, but as so often happens in life it all turned out quite differently.

At the end of my first term Miss Baker, the Head of the Classics Department, was offered a Headship for the September term. Miss Wakeman, who could indeed spring surprises, sent for me and told me that I could not therefore go to the Training College. 'Because,' she added, 'I want you for the Head of the Department here.'

She told me that she had already communicated with Miss Wood, the Head of the Training College, that I must regard my teaching in the school as training and that she would have an inspector to test my practical work at the end of the year and would give me two days off to take the written examinations. So I just said, 'Yes, Miss Wakeman,' and never regretted it. I am not in the least inclined to sit down calmly under orders, but she was so reasonable and frank that somehow everyone was inclined to say, 'Yes, Miss Wakeman.'

The school and its playing fields stood at the top of Chatham Hill adjoining Gillingham and on the main road to the then very attractive village of Rainham. On the opposite side of the main road were many roads leading to the orchards, where in spring the apple and cherry blossom abounded and one could look across the open space called 'The Lines' where there were huts which had been put up during the war—now, alas, replaced by buildings. But in those bygone days one could enjoy a sense of space and see riders enjoying exercise. The school was a very sound, good building and the girls had ample space for games. After school I sometimes used to play rounders with them, the only time I ever really enjoyed an outdoor game. Probably this was because I always have found running easier than walking.

I saw less of the beauty of the countryside during my first term, for my mother had arranged for me to live with a very pleasant widow in the Cathedral Close. Perhaps she was right, for I quickly made many lifelong friends in Rochester. These were Bishop and Mrs. Harmer and their daughter, Adeline. She introduced me to Dean Storrs' family and made me a member of the Girls' Diocesan Association, and I can never say how much this meant, for there were so many of us who did much together. Monica Storrs was not much involved with us then, being older, but what an outstanding person she has always been, in England and in Canada! Amongst the many who met regularly to study and discuss were Adeline, Petronella Storrs and Clare Latham. The last lived with her parents in Dickens' old house, Gadshill. How lovely were the flowers in the garden and in the woods. How often we picnicked in the woods at Cobham too on Lord Darnley's estate. Dorothy Eyres, another of the group, was a great friend and so were her parents. I can never say what I owe to Admiral and Mrs. Eyres, or be thankful enough for the advice he used to give me right up to the time of his death, after the Second World War.

Chatham

Since Admiral Eyres had so much influence on my life I think that my memoirs would be incomplete without a special mention of him. As I have implied, from the time that Dorothy and I made friends in 1919 he and his wife always welcomed me to their home. He was tall and distinguished, with the blue eyes of a sailor. He was, too, a great individualist and a great patriot. When the First World War broke out in 1914 he had just retired from the active list, but wanted to return to the Fleet. Being told that he was above retiring age he promptly joined the army! This posed quite a problem to the authorities and accordingly he was recalled to serve again in the navy in his proper rank of Admiral and gave distinguished service in the Gallipoli campaign. Mrs. Eyres also was a fascinating person; she had a lovely complexion, and like him, had much dignity and grace and had an excellent brain.

From the time when, on his advice, I went to Canada I always kept in touch with them both and visited them on my holidays, even after they had moved to Wimbledon. I well remember once driving with them in a victoria around Richmond Park, to the amusement of people who passed us. Then once—on this occasion when I was back in England for good—I stayed with them, taking Jester and Mickey. I can't remember why I had to take the dogs but they had said it was all right. They loved animals and always had a cat. One of these, Whiskers, had in fact had great experiences at sea with his master.

Alas, during the last war their house was hit by a bomb and Mrs. Eyres was killed although the Admiral tumbled through the house in his bed unharmed. Typical of him, he moved to a top flat in Ashley Gardens and, on one of my holidays during the war, I spent the night there. And what a night! It was one of the heaviest blitz nights that London suffered. I got up and went to see what was happening, but the Admiral called from his room, 'Is that you, Pop? Don't fuss.' Feeling an abject coward I returned to bed.

The last time I saw him, after the war, he had moved to

Putney with the faithful Sarah who had been with him and Mrs. Eyres for so many years. How very grateful one has to be for such friends! It was he and Mrs. Eyres who interested me in French history and French biographies and every bit of conversation with them was interesting, as they had both read so much and remembered so much from their wide field of experience.

At the beginning of my second term at Chatham I left my lodgings with my hostess because, much as I liked her, I felt rightly or wrongly that she did not really approve of career women who earned their living; and this in the year 1919! Also I went up to Westfield most weekends in order to attend a most helpful and stimulating course of lectures, given on Saturdays by Professor Adams of the College of Education. This was not approved of, as much the cheapest way (2s 6d return) was to go up to Town via Gravesend and across the ferry to Tilbury. From my point of view nothing could have been simpler; for every single time either a sailor or a soldier took me under his wing on my return journey and escorted me back to my digs, after having looked after me on the crossing with real old-fashioned courtesy. Once, later, when I was in Gillingham, a sailor entrusted to me a small and delightful monkey to keep until he returned overseas again. It was a darling but it was regarded with severe distrust by my landlady and not popular, except with the girls, when I once took him to school, although he behaved beautifully in class.

I first moved to a room over a small sweetshop in the Maidstone Road in Rochester, and all went well until one night when the owners were out and a kind sailor borrowed a ladder from another shop to let me in at the window of my own room upstairs. The landlady, who would never let me have a key, objected, and told me I had better move. She said it was undignified for a lady to climb a ladder. What should I have done? Walk up and down the road? Go to visit friends at 9 p.m. on a Sunday? When I told Miss Wakeman, she said that she thought I should be nearer the school and not have the long uphill bicycle ride every morning, and she found me nice rooms with a view, and a landlady who let me exercise her dog. I was sad not to be in Rochester, but as Kitty Irvine, whose father was Commandant of the Garrison, came in the same direction, we used to walk home together from G.D.A. meetings and discuss the subjects brought up at the meetings. My life out of school was as happy as it was in school. Occasionally I used to go to Garrison, R.E. or Naval Barrack dances, these last under the direction of Admiral Sturdee.

To return to the school itself, I was so fortunate to be under such a good disciplinarian as Miss Wakeman. She passed nothing that was below standard. The first time I handed her in a list of the thirty-five girls in the form she was at the door of her room with it in her hand at the end of a lesson and, smiling, gave it to me with the remark:

'Do Westfield students always make crooked lists?'

How well she knew each of us! She never again had an untidy list from me, however many times I had to do it. At the end of the first term I had to write duplicate reports for all the form as one copy was sent back to the child's primary school. When she came to sign mine in the staff-room at 5 p.m. she quietly tore them in two and said they must be done tidily. This was a blow, but deserved. I wanted to go home the next day for the holidays, but naturally did not say so. At 10 p.m. or after she arrived at my lodgings to see if I had re-done them, and nobly sat down to sign them all. This was typical of her, for she combined rigid standards with great kindness and understanding. I can never be sufficiently grateful for all she taught me nor for the joy of having her friendship more and more over the four and a half years I was in the school.

Feelings of nervous strain and tenseness were perhaps my principal disadvantages in those early days. Just as I used to lose my head in examinations, so I did in my early days in teaching. I had only been at Chatham for some ten days when a school inspector walked into an English class which I was taking with my own form.

'What subject is this?' he asked as he took a seat.

'Latin,' said I, overcome by confusion.

'English,' whispered the form very quietly.

They were wonderful! We were in fact reading and studying Pope's translation of *The Iliad*. One girl got up in form and did a short reading, while others asked questions. In fact they did their best to carry me through. I gathered afterwards that the inspector had commented to Miss Wakeman that I must be slightly mad; but she had told him that he should have listened from outside.

Later in the same term Miss Wakeman herself came in to listen to a sixth-form composition lesson and again I lost my head and started doing stupid things. However, she went out quietly without comment. The following week we had our usual lively and chatty satisfactory lesson, then when the bell rang we had to end and, to my immense surprise, Miss Wakeman emerged from a cupboard at the back of the room! Then, when the girls had gone, she exclaimed, 'Excellent!' I did not have to bother any more. She really was a splendid psychologist and I gradually got over my nervousness.

Even to this day I am far more happy and at home in a classroom than anywhere else.

I think that it was due to her that we were such a happy staff and the girls were so happy and hard-working. I remember the two delightful staff who taught gymnastics and games; the History mistress with whom I enjoyed many walks and discussions; Miss Evans, Head of English, whom I have since met at Headmistresses meetings; the Domestic Science teacher, Miss Coombes, who taught the juniors; and, very clearly, Miss Roper who had been there a long time and always delighted in reading Ethel M. Dell. This always caused me inner amusement, but she was such a kind and conscientious member of staff. There were others too and how I should like to see them all again.

As for the girls, I was devoted to so many of them and am most grateful to the ones who have always kept up with me. I began by being the form mistress of thirty-five girls who had just come on as scholars from the primary schools. They were intelligent and gay and reasonably naughty. I remember my first taste of this. One morning in the first week I opened my desk to get out the register; I had vaguely wondered why so many of the form were there particularly early, but I found out at once when I saw on the register five dead mice. Looking round I could see who were in suppressed giggles and very pink. So I removed the mice quietly and said nothing. As soon as I had led the form into Prayers I slipped back and put them into the desk of the girl I suspected. When we all came back from Prayers and the child opened her desk and saw the mice there was a great burst of laughter, so that Miss Wakeman looked in. I just said, 'I'm sorry,' and she went out. From that moment the form and I knew each other, and I always enjoyed teaching them English and Latin.

I liked the arrangement of each member of staff taking her own form right up the school. One got to know them well. Also I taught Latin throughout the school and so came into contact with most girls. There was a small group who learnt Greek in order to read Classics at the university. I remember Dorothy Kenyon and Ella Russell who went on to Westfield College, as did Kathleen Staines, who later became Head of the Clergy Daughters' School at Darley Dale, and one clever girl, Doris Simms, who went on to Oxford. Since my retirement I have visited Kathleen's school for Speech Day and was delighted with the atmosphere there. Dorothy, now Mrs. Yarnold, is teaching and lecturing in Freetown, Sierra Leone. She has always kept up with me and I also remember her mother who was a friend of Miss Wakeman and whom I often saw in connection with her being the founder of the Women's Citizens Association, whilst her father was Principal of the Technical School and then of the Gillingham Grammar School.

Apart from class I used to see some of the girls at Guide Meetings, which I took in those days, and others when I took them on expeditions to Rochester Castle and places of historic interest. I have always loved Kent from the time the family moved to Tatsfield, and we used to go to Westerham on bicycles or in the donkey cart. Everywhere there were lovely spots and in particular so much beauty and colour.

After I had finished my course in London and no longer went to Westfield on Saturdays I used to enjoy myself with my friends in Rochester. In our excursions we scoured large portions of Kent and on one occasion we managed to cycle to Whitstable and on another went by train to Dover. Except when the weather was really bad, Kent always seemed to have colour and beauty. Chatham itself was an ugly town but despite that I never really disliked it. Rochester, of course, had its beautiful cathedral with its Close. It also had St. Margaret's Church where Sybil Thorndike's father had been rector until a short while before my own arrival, and people were still speaking with pride of the time when she had started her career by acting at the local theatre. Strood, too, across the River Medway was a pleasant little place and the vicar used to give excellent lectures which we attended.

Somehow there seemed to be more time in those days for what one wanted to do. My first year I spent the whole of my spare time reading for my Teacher's Diploma, but after that I think that I read more novels than ever again in my life, for we had a good lending library where one could browse and get what one wanted whether in the line of novels, travel books or biography.

My urge to travel abroad during the holidays was already on me. At first there was not much money for travelling, but when the Burnham scale was adopted I felt quite rich. So I proposed to Dorothy Eyres that we should take a cheap crossing to Belgium. She agreed with alacrity and Mrs. Eyres said that, as I had done some travelling, she could agree. Dorothy was the youngest of the three daughters and not yet married. I think it was in 1922. How powerful mothers were in those days! Petronella Storrs asked me to go to tea with her mother. Knowing that she was very formidable, I put on my best coat and skirt and thought that I looked respectable, but when I mentioned that Dorothy and I were going to Belgium, she shattered me by saying, 'Well, I suppose it is better to spend your money on travel than on dress.' The attitude and authority of parents has changed since that time! All the same, I question if there is more family affection now than there was then: certainly there is much less respect.

Dorothy and I had a delightful time in Bruges all amongst the Memlincs and on the canals. It was a week of glorious spring weather and the canals had not yet grown smelly as they do in summer, trees were sprouting, flowers were coming out and being sold in the streets, and everything seemed to glitter in the sun, including the clock of the famous *Belfroi*. We then visited Ghent and on Sunday afternoon went on to Brussels where we were horrified to discover that there was an international Fair and every hotel was consequently packed. After a long and fruitless search, and having found that the British Embassy was not open, we called at the police station. The Belgian police were very kind, but when we overheard their phone call begging the only landlady with a vacant room not to let us meet the *danseuses* and to get the room as clean as possible, we did not feel like accepting this particular hospitality. Accordingly, we took a taxi to the English Church and were lucky at 10 p.m. to run into a chorister who led us to the chaplain. Fortunately, the latter had known Admiral and Mrs. Eyres and knew too of my family. So all was well and they found us accommodation in a Girls' Friendly Society hostel.

We spent only a day and a half in Brussels, which did not attract us very much. My chief memory of it being that it had the noisiest trams I have ever heard. We were astounded at the crowds filling the confectioners' shops which were filled with the most luscious-looking cream buns. However, we moved on to Louvain, still a beautiful place with its Cloth Hall, even after its partial destruction by the Germans. The town still had its fourteenth-century atmosphere and reminded us of the great Erasmus who taught in the university and of Thomas More, who wrote his *Utopia* there.

Boring—Never!

It was in 1922 that I received a letter from Miss Knox inviting me to go out to Havergal College in Toronto. I describe in my next chapter how I accepted the post, but I said that I could not go until September 1923, for I felt that, after all her kindness to me, I must give Miss Wakeman long notice to fill my post.

That last year in Chatham seemed to go all too fast. I had learned so much and had put so much into my work that I was very sorry to leave both staff and girls, and friends outside. I had studied and tried out various methods. Some schools at that time were trying out the direct method of teaching Latin, but to me this did not seem very suitable; so that I compromised and got musical girls and staff to set some of Catullus and other poems to music, and after school hours we used to have periods for singing them. That they enjoyed them was, I think, proved, for when I went back to a reunion in the 1950s, to my joy a group of my old girls, then women either married or in jobs, had united to sing to me all those same songs. That to my mind was just typical of Chatham girls. They were always faithful to friends and thorough in their work. They got very good results in their examinations, which in those days were the General and Higher Certificates. When they left school, imbued with the spirit that Miss Wakeman had created throughout, they went on with ambition and determination to universities, to become pupil teachers, to posts of various kinds and some, like E. Dutton, went overseas. She, instigated by me, went under the auspices of the Maple Leaf Fellowship to teach in Saskatchewan. There she was so happy that she married and settled in Canada. Up until the last war I used to hear from her.

I was sad when my time came to leave Miss Wakeman and the school, and my Rochester friends. Yet I realised that I could, without losing my friends, launch out into the wider world.

CHAPTER FOUR

HAVERGAL COLLEGE, TORONTO

⋄⋄⋄

Miss Knox, Headmistress of Havergal College, Toronto, and my beloved Admiral Eyres were the main influences in my move from Chatham to Canada. Miss Richardson at Westfield, in fact, had been asked by Miss Knox to recommend teachers and, amongst others, she had suggested me. When, however, Miss Knox wrote to me inviting me to teach English I wrote to thank her but declined the offer. I neither wanted to teach this subject nor to go to Canada.

However, Miss Knox was not so easily thwarted. She wrote me an amazingly chatty reply which quite gave the impression of its coming from a lively young person and invited me to lunch at the Evangelical Alliance in Stafford Place on her forthcoming visit to London. In the meantime, I had consulted Admiral Eyres and he had told me that one should never lose the opportunity of seeing something of the world and that anyway one must 'always follow the star'. Accordingly, in the end, I accepted the invitation.

On my arrival at the Club a month later I was shown into a room where there was an elderly lady reclining on a sofa. She had white hair and wore a long black dress. I supposed her to be the person in charge of the Club.

'I want to see Miss Knox, please,' I said rather anxiously.

She replied in sepulchral tones:

'Miss Knox!'

'Yes, please,' I shouted, thinking her to be deaf.

In an equally deep voice, she announced:

47

'I am Miss Knox.'

I have never been good at hiding my feelings and certainly must have shown my astonishment, but unperturbed she went on:

'Come in! I suppose that you are comparing me with your present headmistress—and that unfavourably.'

'Well! Yes!' I admitted, truthfully but with some embarrassment. However, she laughed heartily and suggested we should lunch.

Over the meal I was offered the post of English Mistress at Havergal for that year, which was 1922. I explained, as patiently as I could, that it was not English but Classics which I wanted to teach, and that, as Miss Wakeman had taken me straight from university and had already appointed me head of the Classics department, I could not possibly think of leaving her that year. I pleaded that it was only right for me to give her a year's notice, so that she could find a new Head of Classics. To my delight Miss Knox agreed with this and said that I could go out to her the following year and be Head of Classics.

I thought of the Admiral's words, 'follow the star', and accepted. She offered me a paid passage both ways provided I stayed two years; but I did not want to promise this. I little guessed then that I should not leave until after nearly seven years, and then with the utmost regret.

*　　*　　*　　*　　*

The year I went to Havergal, I was one of twenty-one new staff members and many of us travelled out together on the ship. For me, it was the first of twenty or more crossings of the Atlantic, and my mode of travel was to range from steerage to first class.

How fortunate I was that my first sight of Canada was in a September when there had been an early frost that had already turned the trees to their startling reds and browns. We sailed up the St. Lawrence River in glorious sunny weather, so that on

3. Speech Day, Westonbirt School

4. The Author, 1932, with Mickey and Jester

our arrival we had a clear view of Quebec lying high on the northern shore with the arresting sight of the Château Frontenac Hotel towering above the river, then further along the steep cliffs up which Wolfe had climbed to the Heights of Abraham to win his famous victory over the French General Montcalm. From there on to Montreal we saw the maple trees all along the banks, flame-coloured and beautiful beyond description. At a later date I was to visit friends in Montreal and Quebec, visit the Thousand Islands and make acquaintance with many of the small places along the St. Lawrence and on the Richelieu River, but I am glad that I saw those maples in their autumn glory on my first visit.

By the time we had disembarked at Montreal and I had found my place on the train to Toronto I was already feeling desperately home-sick. I was, however, cheered by the lively sound of the train bell. At first, this feature of the North American railways, which since then has become familiar to all cinema-goers, surprised me. Indeed, I even wondered if the sound, which of course manifested itself as we arrived and departed from each station, came from the small churches which were the prominent feature of every place at which we stopped. Beyond this, what impressed me was the space and the size of everything that surrounded me. Everything in Canada seemed so large and spacious, even the station at Montreal with its black-faced porters with their red caps, and the train itself which was so huge in comparison with our English ones. It was only on my first return to England that I fully realised why Canadians would say that English fields were like large green handkerchiefs. In the clear air of Canada even the moon and the stars seemed bigger than at home—and indeed more beautiful.

Miss Knox had herself founded Havergal College some thirty-five years previously, and by the time I went there it was as famous as its friendly rival, Bishop Strachan's School. Moreover, from Havergal, a whole line of girls' public schools had been founded by staff trained by her. These schools spanned the

Canadian continent, all the way from Montreal to Vancouver. By this time, however, Miss Knox herself was becoming elderly and the only active part she was able to take in the life of the school was to play the organ for Prayers. I shall never forget the first day of term. Prayers were in the big hall and the staff sat on the steps of the platform facing the girls when Miss Knox gave out the hymn, 'Number 238—"As pants . . ." ' This sounded so funny that I barely suppressed a hoot of merriment.

At first I hated everything.

To begin with, although I had been promised that I should live in a staff house, I found myself in a small room with only a matchboard partition between myself and the girls' cubicles. Highly indignant, after a very short time I sought out Miss Knox to protest, and was much surprised and amused to find her in bed wearing purple and white striped pyjamas and with a long tail of her white hair on the table beside her. However, she was sympathetic to my complaint and said that I could, if I wished, move into a house across the garden. First, however, she told me that I must speak to Miss Jessie Dykes, who was then head of the Boarders.

Jessie Dykes was a delightful and determined person; small, quiet, dignified, a brilliant teacher of English, beloved and respected by staff and girls. From that very first meeting until the day of her death at seventy-five, we enjoyed a close and wonderful friendship. I explained to her that I did not want to live in a boarding school.

She replied quietly but obliquely:

'Do you truly want to have some influence with the young and help them?'

'Most certainly I do!' I replied.

'All right, then,' she said, smiling kindly, 'don't move.'

What could one do?

There was yet another thing which made me even more angry. Miss Knox had promised that I would be in charge of Classics, but I found to my consternation that Miss Wood, the Vice-Principal, was already in charge. Unexpected developments sorted this out later on, but at the time I was very disgruntled. Despite these disadvantages, I was, however, allowed complete freedom to teach according to my own methods; and this gave me a measure of satisfaction.

Moreover, I was not the only rebel. Amongst the new staff quite a number were also rather insubordinate. I remember the occasion when a friend and I were in the staff-room where we did our corrections. With us in the room was also a Miss Lange. Everyone suspected that she, who had long been on the staff, was a tale-bearer and reported to Miss Knox everything that went on, or any conversation which could be considered out of place. The young member of the science staff, who was with me that day, and I decided we would find out, once and for all. With this in mind, she said to me:

'What shall we do tonight to enliven our existence? Any ideas?'

She spoke this in an audible whisper and I whispered my reply equally loudly:

'Let's go up on the roof and smoke,' I suggested, and pointed the remark with a guilty giggle.

Both these activities were strictly forbidden and the sequel was laughable in the way it immediately fulfilled our expectations. Two minutes later, Miss Lange left the room and in five minutes Miss Knox's bell rang. I was requested to go to her bedroom to see her. To my surprise, she greeted me pleasantly.

'What are you doing with yourself this evening?' she asked nonchalantly.

Much amused, I said:

'I don't know yet, Miss Knox, but I do know for certain I am not going up on the roof and I am not going to smoke.'

At this she roared with laughter.

'So-ho! You've got Miss Lange taped, have you?'

Miss Knox, who could never resist a joke, the following week said that Miss Lange was going to hear an interesting Englishman who was touring Canada, and suggested I went with her. Little did I suspect that I was to be taken to a huge church to hear a famous evangelistic preacher. We had an emotional hymn followed by a long sermon, punctuated every now and then by the appeal: 'Those who are saved please stand up.' Each time Miss Lange stood and I remained seated. I think this was just a practical joke engineered by Miss Knox.

There remained yet another bone of contention between the Principal and myself. She told me I must attend St. Paul's Church. This I refused to do. I did not like St. Paul's and said so. I continued to go to St. James's.

As a result of all these contretemps and disagreements, I blew up one day and gave in my written resignation.

I might have spared myself the pains. All the notice Miss Knox took was merely to tear it up. In a voice, faintly touched with laughter but which plainly would accept no denial, she said:

'You certainly won't want to go back to England! It is equally certain I won't let you go to any of the private schools* in Canada—you see, I know all the headmistresses! And, you can't go to a State school because you haven't got the Ontario Teachers' Certificate. So that would seem to be that.' She smiled benignly and dismissed the matter.

This did not suit me at all. Although I had both affection and admiration for Miss Knox, I went on fighting for my individual freedom. On the Saturday following my attempted resignation, I went to the Parliament building to try to see the Minister of Education. I wanted to ask if it were possible for me to take the Ontario Teachers' Certificate. I could not see him that day, but I went the following week and explained the whole situation to him. He knew Miss Knox well and was most amused and sympathetic. He said he would find some way out for me, and told me to go the following week to see the Dean of the College of Education. To him, I had to explain that I could not attend lectures as my teaching left me free on Saturdays only. The Dean also was most understanding and helpful. As I had the Cambridge Diploma, he allowed me to sign up for the lectures.

* The equivalent of English Public Schools.

Havergal

In addition, when I could fit it in, I was free to see any of the professors, and hence to take the examination.

Then at Christmas, to change everything, Miss Knox died. I found out that, in the new conditions, there were doubts being expressed by the Dean and members of the College of Education as to whether I would go on with my attempt to take the Certificate or not. In fact there was a bet on it amongst my friends. That made no difference, however, for I had decided to go on to take the exam in any case.

The written papers were not difficult but the course covered all kinds of subjects, including hygiene: and I had to give the only geography lesson of my life. Also, the examination included taking a class of boys in Latin. Over this I quite unconsciously caused no little amusement. On the blackboard was chalked the professor's method of teaching gerunds and gerundives. Saying that I had a better one, I cheerfully rubbed this off and proceeded to expound my own. I had completely forgotten that my lesson was part of the exam, but everyone must have been kind and lenient, for I got a 98% Certificate.

On the whole the girls at Havergal were a grand lot—I liked most of them immensely although those in the matriculation class were, compared with English girls, more sophisticated, though far behind in standard of learning compared with the English; many of them seemed more grown up than I was. Very naughtily, but naturally, they made a point of trying to lead staff newly out from England a rare dance.

I shall never forget my first Latin lesson. They behaved abominably—they talked; they ate huge slices of bread and butter; they cracked nuts with the utmost noise possible. Finally, several of them sang out in chorus: 'We don't wish to go on with rotten old Latin!'

At that I looked at them with all the indifference I could muster.

'Very well, then,' I said, 'I shall write my letters until you are ready to be taught.'

While all this was happening, Miss Knox passed along the corridor.

'Now! You'll get into a row,' they all sang out.

'On the contrary,' I replied with emphasis, 'but you may!'

As I had expected, the next day all was peace.

I took them off their dreadful 'Ontario Latin Book' and taught them *Latin*, and we all enjoyed ourselves. In fact it worked too well for, after a time, some of the girls in the senior class pretended they were not good enough for that class and kept on being sent down to my class. We all but overflowed into the passage. Fortunately, they all did very well in their examinations—even without their 'Ontario Latin Book'; and a group of them went on to read Classics at the university.

Owing to the hot summer, as elsewhere on the American continent, Christmas and Easter holidays at Havergal were short; and this allowed for a school year running right through from 8th September to 8th June. This provided a long summer vacation—long enough to allow for extensive travel, and essential for English staff who wanted to go home for the summer in the days before aeroplanes.

I had decided to go to England this first summer holiday, little guessing the responsibility which was to be thrust upon me as the result of Miss Knox's death. No decision had yet been made concerning her successor and, for this reason, neither Miss Wood nor Miss Dykes wished to be absent from Canada that summer, but twenty-one new members of staff had to be engaged in England and the responsibility was given to me. Needless to say I was appalled at the prospect. To appoint staff for a school one is not running is no easy task, but, fortunately, teachers were not so hard to get then as now and my selection was approved. When I had completed this assignment, I joined my friend Adeline Harmer, with whom I then went to Rome.

Eventually, Miss Wood became Headmistress and Miss Dykes her second-in-command. To my surprise and pleasure I was made head of the Boarders.

In April 1926, when I had been at Havergal for about three years and was enjoying my work, which incidentally meant enjoying myself as well, the foundations were laid for a new school building. Because Jarvis Street, where Havergal was then situated, had become so absorbed into the commercial area of Toronto, the Council decided to build a new section of the school further out on the north side in Lawrence Park.

We moved in during September. Miss Wood remained in charge of Jarvis Street, and Miss Dykes became head of Lawrence Park, where I was her deputy. It was a beautiful building, in neo-Gothic style, and at that time it was situated in the open country, with its gardens surrounded by fields. From my window I had a wide view of a large open space in the middle of which was a solitary tree. There was a ravine just beyond the garden on the north side, which was haunted by beautiful birds such as the tiny, scarlet Cardinal bird and Bobolinks with their delightful song. In the garden, I was allowed to erect a pole with a dovecot on top which afforded me much pleasure. Later, so I was told after I had left, it had to be taken away, as its winged population became too numerous.

Finally, as far as animals are concerned, joy of joys, I was allowed to keep a dog. Someone gave me a darling, wire-haired, terrier puppy. He was called Jester and he spent the rest of his fifteen years with me.

One incident of Jester's life which has always fascinated me to recall, is his story of true love. It started one day when he was out with the French Mistress—Mademoiselle Favre. He met a Boston Bull Terrier, Mickey, and evidently she fell deeply in love with him, for from that moment her owners could never keep her at home. No matter what they did, she would escape and flee across the fields to join Jester. When they came to fetch her, which they did repeatedly, the clever Mickey seemed to sense their presence and crept away and hid herself. On one such an occasion, thinking she had gone home, I told her owners I had not seen her. Later, I discovered a large warm bump in my bed, and there was Mickey cuddled under the eiderdown to hide and Jester was sitting beside her on guard. Eventually her owners decided to sell her to me and she and

Jester passed many happy years together. Both came to Jersey with me, and from there on to Westonbirt. There Mickey died. I only had Jester when I moved to Cheltenham.

When we first moved in to Lawrence Park, the grounds and approach paths were not yet completed. It was a particularly wet September and the earth was sodden. We had to reach the building by way of duckboards placed over the mud; but we were all so happy in our new home that we did not mind in the least.

I spent three and a half years at Lawrence Park and every one of them was a real joy to me. I look back now with the happiest memories on the whole of the school life, the staff and the girls—also with affectionate memories of the numerous friends I made in Toronto.

Amongst those friends who stand out most vividly was Victoria Rossiter, the Vice-Principal of Bishop Strachan's School and an old Cheltonian. She did much to help to settle me during my first term in Canada. Again, there was Agatha Cassells. She had many English connections and became a staunch friend, as was her sister, Peggy Dale-Harris. Her daughter, Agatha, learnt Greek with me at the age of eight, before she came permanently as a day girl to the school. Her grandmother, Mrs. Dale-Harris, was also a treasured friend. She was a wonderful old lady who, at the age of eighty, learnt Hebrew. She lived in Ottawa and I spent several Christmas holidays with her while I was in Canada.

Ottawa was entrancing, especially the part at Hull where the Ottawa River joined the Rideau Canal and the whole junction was filled with lumber they had floated down from the forests of the north. At Christmas the city itself was beautiful under the snow, and the Parliament buildings on the cliff edge of the river gave wide and beautiful views. The War Memorial depicting active members of the fighting forces, with animal life including horses, mice and other creatures, in my mind surpasses even the one in Edinburgh.

During the first winter after my arrival in Canada, I went

with a friend to spend the weekend on the American side of Niagara. We spent a day on the Canadian side which was the more beautiful. It has to be seen to be believed: and in those days it was natural beauty without coloured lights or anything else to spoil it. I shall never forget those torrents, with the spray making a great frozen pile beneath; and the trees, every twig covered with ice so that the branches tinkled in the wind. Of course after that I saw it in spring and summer. Always it was entrancing, but never more so than on that sunny winter's day.

On the Sunday we went to the Episcopalian Church on the American side. After the service with its too-long sermon by a parson with a ghastly accent, he hurried after us as we were going out and asked me where we had come from.

'Toronto,' I said.

'Oh,' said he, 'but surely England, I imagine, by your twang!'

The visits I paid to Lake Simco where the Woods had a house are unforgettable; and also those to the Bruin's house on Stoney Lake, where for the first time I heard that queer cry of the loons, almost like a siren. It was hard to see the birds themselves, for they swim so far under water. Once, too, I went to Georgian Bay, the large inlet off Lake Huron, where the inhabitants had houses on the numerous islands.

One of the joys of Canada was that it opened up to me a new literature, Canadian and American. Canadian history may be short, but the early life of this great country was fascinating. I read the histories of the days of colonisation with immense interest. Louis Hémon's novel *Maria Chapdelaine* inspired interest in the pioneer colonists of Lake St. John. The North American novelists showed the life of Main Street, not only that of Gopher Prairie, Minnesota, in Sinclair Lewis's famous book, but all those others we saw in the Middle West of Canada and America. There was Thornton Wilder of *The Bridge of San Luis Rey*, then Willa Catha and Mazo de la Roche with her vivid accounts of the Anglo-Irish family in the Niagara peninsula. As we walked the dogs, Jessie and I had fascinating discussions of both

Canadian and English books of the time; and I enjoyed, too, walking with Grace Wetherhead, our good historian, who in my early days there pointed out how here and there one saw remains of early settlers' huts near new sophisticated buildings, and so on.

Canada has an air of energy and growth, of a still excitingly developing country. I'm glad I was there in the 1920s and not in the 60s. I feel the same about the States, too. When I was in Rochester, State of New York, the new Kodak town was fresh and growing and even in Washington with the flowering Japanese cherry trees along the Potomac there was a sense of peace.

Back in Toronto, many Sundays were reserved for a happy time with Canon and Mrs. Bruin at their delightful home. He was Vicar of St. Simon's Church. I taught their daughter, Rosalind, at Havergal and still see her sometimes, now that she is married and lives in London. Then there were Douglas and Aileen Wood, whose friendship I have always kept up, and with whom I stayed when I went back to visit friends in 1950. I cannot feel too grateful for the hospitality I met with all the way along from the parents of the girls I taught, and from the old girls themselves after they had left.

There were some very outstanding girls at Havergal during my time: Jean Lang, Isabel and Gwethlyn Brown, Drummond Fraser from Alabama, whose two daughters Wendy and Gillian Dumeresque were with me at Cheltenham later on; and Catherine Steele, who taught history for a year at Westonbirt, and who is now the Principal of Havergal College. There are so many whom I remember and should love to see again.

Havergal was not only a happy school; it was a school with breadth of vision. Not only was the teaching the girls received first class, but on Saturdays there were also interesting and exciting expeditions. Some Saturdays in winter, I went out sledging with the girls, and once we rode in an iceboat on the lake: there was also the annual skating tournament. In addition to these gay pastimes Saturday excursions had their serious, cultural counterpart—equally as enjoyable—such as trips to lectures, concerts and art exhibitions in the town.

* * * * *

One Christmas Jessie Dykes and I saw a notice advertising a cheap, nine-day trip to Florida for people wanting to buy real estate. We went along to the office of the agents and explained that we were school teachers, that we neither could nor would buy any land, but that we would love to go on the train, if we might. With the spontaneous generosity of the Canadian, they said, yes, we could go.

And did they do us in style? They gave us a drawing-room compartment on the train and made sure that we had everything we wanted. It was exciting leaving the cold and the blizzards of a Toronto winter for gentler climes, and in due course we found ourselves winding southwards through North and South Carolina, then through Georgia with the weather every day becoming perceptibly hotter. Here we saw, for the first time, the Spanish moss hanging, like giants' beards, from the trees. To arrive in Florida, so soon after leaving the bitter northern winter, was a unique experience—it seemed unbelievable; but there were more wonders in store. Although the estate people had been duly warned that we had not come to buy, a kind land-owner took us around in his car to see the various sights of Florida and to visit the famous bird sanctuary.

I was particularly thrilled by this as it was the creation of Edward Bok whose life I had read. He took us over it personally and invited us into his house and garden. We had a long conversation in which he told me of his early life as a barefooted boy in New York, and how from selling papers he had taught himself to write: thanks to this, accompanied by his business ability, he had amassed a fortune and retired to Florida—a State which was then little occupied and still retained its primitive beauty—even in mid-winter the water of its lakes was as much as 70° F. Little wonder that these days many Canadians have their annual holidays in the winter and go to Florida.

Boring—Never!

Our most exciting journey, however, was in the summer vacation of 1929, when Jessie and I did a motor tour of ten thousand miles. I had bought a car and learned to drive about six weeks before, and in my Pontiac we headed south. We drove through Detroit and Michigan, on to Denver, and then to Santa Fé to visit friends. New Mexico enthralled us. I was especially impressed with the old Archbishop's Palace at Santa Fé with the tree growing in the centre of it.

From Santa Fé we went across the desert to Albuquerque, excited to see innumerable chipmunks and prairie dogs on the way. We had to drive by night because of the heat during the day. When we arrived at Albuquerque the hotel manager asked if we had seen some very wild Indians on horseback. We said that we had at a moment when we stopped to have a rest and to watch the lovely coloured dragonflies. They rode round us and waved and we could not understand what they said. The manager was amazed, for these same Indians had murdered two people that night!

Another time when we were nearly buried in a sandstorm, two strong men passed and dug us out. Out in the desert we could often find some tiny shack open at 4 a.m. to give us coffee and waffles with maple-sugar. We could nearly live on the fruit which we were allowed to pick up off the ground; for fallen fruit was free.

We spent one night on the Navajo Reservation. Here we slept in cabins which had curtains instead of doors and we left our luggage in the car, without bothering to lock it. The man at the only store had assured us that everything and everyone was quite safe. This was a pleasant surprise after our previous scare about the Indians. Indeed, the Navajo tribe with their horses and their beautiful silver and stone work, their nobility of demeanour, and their honesty, was so unexpected, that it gave us tremendous pleasure. We left the Reservation with regret.

Perhaps our most amazing experience was our drive across the desert from Flagstaff, Arizona, to the Grand Canyon. We had to start before dawn and at that hour everything looked yellow and burnt green, but at sunrise the scene turned to all the colours of the rainbow. I can still see the glorious colours in my mind's eye as we crossed the vast expanse of undeveloped country—in those days that part of the world had not been opened up in the manner it is today. When, at length, we reached the Colorado River it was midnight, but the heat was nonetheless suffocating—the temperature being 106°. But this we were told was nothing! On the previous night it had been ten degrees higher!

It was when we were at Flagstaff that I discovered that Jessie Dykes, in addition to her many virtues and her moral steadfastness, had also immense physical courage. We went for what was meant to be a short drive but got on to a mountain track. On the left there was a rocky wall of about 1,000 ft., and on the right a drop of similar height. We could not turn, for it was too narrow. There was nothing to do but go on. After many miles we came to a place where a boulder had dropped on to the track. Terrified, as there was no alternative, I had to squeeze past. There was not an inch to spare and the car hovered, but we passed. I drove a short way and stopped as my knees were shaking. Only then did Jessie speak and move. Were it not for her courage and control we should never have passed, of that I'm sure. That 'short drive' was indeed a long one, for the canyon went on for 150 miles and as darkness overtook us we decided to wait until dawn, not knowing what might be in front. When daylight appeared we saw a huge grizzly bear calmly looking at us from above. Then after the canyon we encountered a man who told us the best way back to Flagstaff, to the kindly hotel people who were anxious about us, and to a good, sound sleep.

The Grand Canyon itself is too remarkable for me to venture a description. It fully lived up to all I had heard and read of its strange beauty. After staying the night on its rim we left in the morning for Pasadena, where we were given hospitality by Gladys Poignand and a friend who lived there. She was on the

Havergal staff when I arrived and stayed on until she eventually joined me in Jersey and at Westonbirt.

From Pasadena we drove up the coast of California, calling at numberless places on the way, such as Santa Barbara and Santa Monica, and thence to San Francisco. I understand that it is quite a different world around there these days and that everything has changed a great deal since 1930, but at that time there was so much that was wild and unspoiled. I am glad that I was able to see so much before I left Canada for good. Whilst I was in California, I had my one and only experience of earning dollars, other than by teaching. I went peach canning! It is a profitable, but not altogether entrancing job.

From there our itinerary now took us, still going north, through the Redwoods, and the time we spent in Yellowstone Park with its geysers and hot springs, its birds and flowering trees is an enduring memory. To an animal lover such as I, naturally the bears and their cubs were the outstanding feature. Finally, we went to Vancouver, then across to Vancouver Island, where we completed our journey by driving down the Nanaimo Pass to Victoria to see our friends.

On the homeward trek the most memorable incident was an adventurous journey along a perilous track through the mountains which eventually landed us in a small town in Montana. Here we had to spend two nights having the brakes and gears serviced. It was a dreary place. There was nothing in the town apart from the main street and the garage, and we felt rather depressed having to stay in a shabby and dismal sort of inn—'a one-horse dump' and no mistake. But there was balm in store to cheer us up. In the evening the girl from the garage came round to invite us to have supper with her family. We spent a pleasant and homely evening. The grandparents had come from Cornwall nearly a century before and now the girl's parents were getting on in life but still loved to hear of England and, before we left, the ancient family Bible was produced in which we had to sign our names. It is this spontaneous hospitality which gives the Middle West its charm.

Yet, on reflection, this was not the only instance when we had been made to feel pleasantly at home. All the way along, we had met with nothing but kindness, help and consideration, so that, eventually, when, after a pilgrimage of ten weeks and ten thousand miles we returned to Havergal, we were filled with a joyous satisfaction.

* * * * *

I had got my trans-continental trip in just in time. For in the autumn of that same year, 1929, I unexpectedly received an invitation to England to be interviewed for a Headship. To this day I have no idea how this invitation materialised, but I suspect that Nora Almond had something to do with it.

Having obtained leave to go, I left the dogs with Jessie and Mademoiselle Favre and ten days later I was in England again, staying with Nora Almond at Bristol from where I travelled to Sherborne to see the Council of that school. Dr. Cyril Norwood, who was an influential member of the Sherborne Council, was also looking for a Head for Jersey College for Girls. It was he who with this in mind persuaded the rest of the Council not to appoint me, for he thought me unsuitable to follow Miss Mulliner, knowing that I might want to make too many changes.

After the meeting in Sherborne I was asked, before returning to Canada, to see the Secretary to the group of schools which had taken over Jersey College.

Thus next day I found myself walking up the path of the vicarage of Monckton Combe, near Bath in Somerset. This was to see the Reverend Percy Warrington, the incumbent, of whom I shall have more to tell in connection with the part he was to play in my life during the subsequent years. It was he who, in his capacity as Secretary of the Trust which was the governing body of the schools, had been mainly responsible for the acquisition of the Jersey College and, as he had not been present at the interview, it was felt essential that I should see him.

Certainly, the rotund little parson with his rosy 'girl's' cheeks, whom I was to meet pacing up and down his study, opposing the finger-tips of his two hands in front of him and tapping one finger against the other as he talked, asked me the most unusual question which I have encountered at any interview.

'How would you teach the first three chapters of Genesis?' he asked abruptly, suddenly stopping in his tracks and looking at me intently.

'According to common sense; wouldn't you?' I replied.

'Quite, quite,' he said.

He had evidently decided that I was to be appointed to Jersey and did not want to start an argument, for he was, I believe, a verbal inspirationalist. I was quite unaware then that he and some of the Governors were so violently Low Church and against a scholarly interpretation of the Old Testament.

I did not want to leave Canada and I did not want, in the least, to go and live on an island. I had thrown so much of myself into my work at Havergal: and, in turn, Havergal had given me so much. My heart was in full-time teaching and I had never really wanted a Headship with its administrative ties. All the same, my attitude has always been that fresh responsibilities bring their own challenge and must not be shirked. And I continued to have in mind my dear friend, Admiral Eyres' message to 'follow the star'. During my last two years in Canada I had acquired two valuable assets that would help me in my new responsibilities. First was the bettered powers of mental organisation that had come from a course in Pelmanism. The other was knowledge from two courses I had taken in Theology. They were both to stand me in good stead.

My new appointment at Jersey College for Girls was to start in March 1930 and I left Havergal in time to take it up. I was cheered by the thought that Gladys Poignard and ten of my Havergal pupils were to join me in April and more of them would be coming in September.

CHAPTER FIVE

JERSEY COLLEGE FOR GIRLS

∞∞

A T THE END of the spring term of 1930, I set off to cross the
Atlantic with Mickey and Jester. We sailed from New
York in the Cunard liner, *Mauretania*—a splendid ship.
By this time I was prepared to face the future even if it involved
abandoning the exciting horizons of a vast continent for the
confines of a tiny island; furthermore, I was looking forward to
keeping my Havergal contacts through the Canadian pupils
who were to join me at the end of the holidays and continue
their education with me in Jersey. I have always thought that
this was very trusting of their parents.

For me it was a fortunate voyage as, owing to the equinoctial
gales being at their height and the reputation the ship had for
rolling and tossing unduly, bookings had not been heavy. For
the same reason the very few first-class passengers there were
remained in their cabins. I was therefore allowed to have the
dogs with me. They had a bunk to themselves and were given
V.I.P. treatment. The stewards, who were exceptionally kind
and attentive in every way, petted them and brought them
excellent meals. As there was a lower deck where it was usually
safe to exercise the dogs, we were all very happy.

A highlight of the voyage for me was meeting Archdeacon
Head who was on his way to a distinguished ecclesiastical
incumbency in Australia. He must, I am sure, have made a
splendid prelate. I remember even now how the inspiring
services, which he held in the lowest lounge, attracted all of
the passengers who could survive the storms.

Boring—Never!

I was favourably impressed with the Jersey College for Girls from the start. The College is a good-looking Georgian building in front and stands high above the town of St. Helier with access by a good road. We could just see the sea, although we were behind the shopping centres and main streets. My personal apartments were two front rooms and I was looked after by kind Mrs. Mortimer, the gardener's wife, and was very comfortable and happy for I always liked to be near the boarders.

The house behind provided classrooms for junior forms and from it there were lanes and small roads all straggling up the hill. The College garden—thanks to Mortimer—grew flowers and many crops; so rich was the soil that we had two crops of potatoes and two of tomatoes annually. In fact the grass of the island is so rich that the cows have to be tethered to prevent them overeating. What attracted me immensely were the valleys of wild spring flowers. At first the island seemed so small that, driving over it, I was almost obsessed with the idea that I might go over the edge, so different was it from the long distances of Canada.

The Jersey College for Girls was one of the schools associated with the Evangelical Foundations that came into existence through the energies of that remarkable man, the Reverend Percy Warrington, whom I have already described on my visit to him at his vicarage at Monckton Combe. One of these unusual characters that break through the surface of our rather stereotyped English life from time to time, the Reverend Percy Warrington, though a person of obscure origins, had during the 1920s crusaded forth from his quiet vicarage to considerable effect. A dynamic personality, an enthusiastic and expert fundraiser, he had not only collected the money, but also established the patronage, both aristocratic, scholastic and clerical to found such well-known schools as Stowe, Westonbirt, Canford and Harrogate that have become features of the educational landscape right down to the present day. With such people as Lord Guisborough as Chairman of the Trust and Dr. Cyril Norwood, Headmaster of Harrow, occupying an important position, one could feel a serene confidence in the future that was unshaken by the bustling activities of Mr. Warrington himself, who had installed himself as Secretary of the Trust.

Jersey College for Girls, an older foundation, had fairly recently been acquired at the time of my appointment and the position when I arrived was that, after two excellent Heads, Miss Roberts first, then Miss D'Auvergne, there had been several short-time holders of the post and a lack of continuity. As I, too, was there so short a time, I was very thankful later on that my successor, Miss Barton, stayed on for many years, including the awful days of the war, when the island suffered so much under the Germans.

The reception I received from Mr. P. N. Richardson who welcomed me was kind and considerate. Mr. Richardson, who was an Advocate of the Royal Court, was head of the local Council of the College and, besides seeing that everything was in order for my take-over, he had the thoughtfulness to arrange good, spacious quarters for the quarantine of my dogs. They were allowed up to twenty visitors a day and there was also a kind old man who gave them walks at night.

In regard to this question of quarantine, there is much to be said for bringing back a dog to Britain *via* Jersey. For one thing, after the dogs have done their six months' quarantine in Jersey, there are no further restrictions for them to enter Britain; and quarantine conditions in Jersey are vastly superior. There are fewer animals taken at a time which allows for more individual attention. Also the site was central, easily accessible and had excellent exercising ground large enough to give a dog a good run playing ball or throwing a stick. I used to visit them for an hour, at least, every morning before work, from 6.30–7.30 a.m.

I have to be grateful, too, to Mr. Richardson, for much more than his thoughtfulness regarding the well-being of my dogs. He made me familiar with much of the history of the island and I visited many of the fascinating places with which the island abounds. One of the places which always captivated me was St. Brelade's Bay. It is a long, shallow bay, dominated by the headland of St. Aubin's to the east. There the little old church is so close to the sea that during early Communion Service one could hear the lap of the wavelets on the sands. The chalice dates back to Queen Elizabeth I and the whole place has a sense of history. There in the early morning—like Yeats—I could feel peace comes dropping slow. Still when I think of St. Brelade's I can hear the water lapping 'in the deep heart's core'.

Then there is Gorey—the little port on the north-east corner of the island, from where on a clear day one could see the French coast thirteen miles away. The view is even better from the ruined battlements of the ancient castle that dominates the harbour. Gorey Castle dates back to the tenth century and was built by Count Robert of Normandy, brother of the Conqueror. From its heights one could look down on the tiny harbour, for all the world just like a toy port with its yachts and fishing boats.

Nor must I forget the historic *Manoir* of St. Ouen's. Since time immemorial this imposing old manor has been in the de Carteret family—*Seigneurs* of St. Ouen's. The Seigneur when I was in Jersey was a delightful person, Reginald Malet de Carteret. He was a Jurat of the Royal Court and a member of the States, governing body of the island. Legend has it that, in ancient days when time was young, St. Ouen's was inhabited by cave dwellers. But Seigneur Reginald was no troglodyte. He was one of the kindest people I have ever met. His kindness was only equalled by that of other islanders. I still treasure the etching of Mont Orgueil Castle, Gorey, by the artist Frank G. Faed and the picture of bluebells in Kew, done and presented to me by Mr. S. G. Blampied. Blampied, Lemaistre, de Gruchy, Le Gallais, Joualt, Le Sueur and Le Rossignol—the nightingale; how charming these names of the old Jersey families—hardly one without memory of some kindness done. How staunch and steadfast they were—both as pupils and friends! They still retained the qualities of the old Huguenot stock which fled to the island from the Cevennes in the days of persecutions of the Protestants.

Jersey

It was easy to settle in the island, for, through the ages Jersey people have travelled and traded all over the world, and hence are tolerant and open-minded. My ex-pupil friend, Marguerite Syvret, now Senior French Mistress and Careers Mistress at Streatham Hill and Clapham High School (Girls Public Day School Trust) has told me that, as early as 1766, the Robin family had its own trading centre in Gaspé Bay, on the shores of the Gulf of St. Lawrence—largely populated by Jersey emigrants. Her own great-grandfather sailed—and I mean *sailed*, round the world seven times, captaining his own ship.

Jersey is not only blessed in her native population, however. She is also fortunate in the quality of the strangers who, for one reason or another, seek her out as an agreeable place of domicile. Amongst them too I made many friends. There was Rear-Admiral C. S. Lewin and his charming wife, whose daughter Peggy came to the College; Colonel H. H. Hulton, D.S.O., who was Government Secretary, and Mrs. Hulton. Their daughter Anne was a real personality. She, too, came to the College and, although greatly handicapped by deafness, kept up in all classes. Then there were Archdeacon and Mrs. Palmer. These two people became friends for life. I had a wonderful Christmas with them in 1938—the last Christmas before the war, and I still look forward to the all too rare visits Mrs. Palmer pays to London. I think of them every time—and that means daily—as I get out the Worcester tea-set they gave me when they stayed with me in Westonbirt, just before I moved to Cheltenham.

When I first took over, the College had already earned a well-merited reputation. But I felt there were many items on the syllabus which I could amplify.

Before, however, I plunge into an account of these strenuous activities, I must recount an amusing incident which established me firmly on the road which I intended to follow. This concerned Mr. Warrington in what I might call a typical example of his behaviour. Amongst certain other things which were unacceptable to me, he was unreasonable enough to insist that

I should take the boarders to a certain, very dull church. I refused to do this and wrote him to that effect.

In reply he sent me this very dictatorial wire: 'Either return to that church or leave the school.'

I received the telegram late in April and replied at once: 'Content. Sail for Canada, 5th May.'

Somehow this lively exchange of sharp shooting became known throughout the island. It caused much excitement and amusement, but my wire had the desired effect. It brought a prompt if terse reply: 'Crossing tonight.'

Then, as I expected, all was settled the way I wanted.

From then on we went to the parish church where Dean Faultes welcomed us and, always after, we could count on him for spiritual help and guidance. There was also a further bonus to that visit. During it I succeeded in extracting from Mr. Warrington a promise that the Council would build for us a much-needed library to celebrate the jubilee of the college which fell in that year. It was, I am pleased to say, completed and opened in the following September. It is a beautiful library and I am glad recently to have heard from Miss Farewell, the present Headmistress, who was for a time a member of my history staff at Cheltenham, that it has now been extended in the same style to take in two more rooms.

I can't remember if it was on this visit, or a later one, that Mr. Warrington, owing to financial disagreements, decided to abolish the local Council of the College. Anyway I do remember that, when documents for this were drawn up, he left these with me and returned to England, leaving me to deal with the matter. This seemed to me a mean trick!

It was when he came over to see about a problem of dry rot in the Junior House, however, that I recollect the incident when, on his tour of the house, he spotted a crucifix in a mistress's private room. He pointed to it with the curt remark, 'She must go.' I made no comment and of course paid no attention.

There was a further episode in connection with Mr.

Warrington's management which occasioned me no small amount of irritation. As we had no bursar at Jersey it was my responsibility to draw the money from our account monthly to pay the tradesmen and other current bills. One month I was dismayed when the bank manager informed me that the whole of our balance had been transferred to Westonbirt. I phoned Mr. Warrington, furiously declaring that if the money was not returned at once I would leave forthwith. It was back next day!

What I felt to be essential to the College was to raise the academic standard, and encourage the girls to think more deeply and never to be content with less than their best. My feelings at that time are, perhaps, best expressed in the following quotation from my report on Speech Day, at the close of the school year in July 1931:

'A vital interest in the outside world must be a salient characteristic of the College if it is to turn out women capable of playing a useful part in this modern world. It yearly becomes more imperative that girls should be educated to have trained minds, adequate knowledge and a wider vision, for in these days, whether they are employers or employed, they have to decide what they think on questions of national import and to form epoch-making decisions never demanded of them in the past.

'The crisis through which the world is passing demands the elimination of the wilfully stupid or idle, and calls for a habit of thoroughness in work and a system of education that trains children, not only to amass knowledge, but also to assimilate it and to use facts as a basis for genuine thought—an education that shall help to turn out men and women who are sincere searchers after truth.

'We ought to give, and you have a right to ask for your daughters, a good grounding in facts (since without knowledge thought is impossible), and a knowledge of those subjects that help to produce clear thought and to develop the critical faculty.

'Above all, we need to develop a religious sense—to teach the practice of the presence of God, so that, in the words of the Collect, "we may have a right judgment in all things".'

It must be recorded that, in achieving these high aspirations, I was immensely helped by Miss Holt, and later by Miss Cheshire. The latter was a historian who came as Second Mistress. Some years later she returned to the island to become Head of the College. Also much credit must be given to Miss Hill and Miss Greenup in charge of the Junior School, where they laid a very sound foundation upon which others could build.

My view is that any school should demand the best possible work from its pupils, but I am well aware that not all girls can be academic. I decided, therefore, that there should be other courses, outside academic fields, open to the older girls. We built up a good Domestic Science Course and a Secretarial Training Course which included languages. On the domestic science side it was possible to train the girls to become nurses, dieticians and other kinds of medical auxiliaries. This enterprise was quickly successful. Before I left I was able to report that several girls had secured good, interesting posts both in England and in Canada.

We also made many innovations so that recreational hours became more interesting and useful. Time off was not wholly devoted to swimming, games and physical culture. The older girls attended lectures in St. Helier. Also they were encouraged to put on plays. In 1931 we were ambitious enough to present *Antigone* and the performances and production were remarkably good.

Due to our proximity to France, inexpensive Continental holidays were easy to arrange. Under the guidance of Miss Holt, a perfectionist in everything and a brilliant teacher, this resulted in numerous girls reaching an exceedingly high standard in French, and teachers of this language from Jersey are to be found in many parts of the world. In the summer of 1930

Miss Poignand took a group of girls to Paris, Strasbourg, Munich and the Passion Play at Oberammergau. At Christmas some stayed in Paris and others went to the winter sports in Switzerland. In the Easter holidays of 1931 a party went to Rome, Pompeii and Florence.

A most satisfactory development, during my term, was the extension and reorganisation of the Junior School. Mont Cantel, as it was called, became a fully fledged preparatory school. The kindergarten—first and second forms—then came into the very capable hands of Miss Balding and the school was run on Froebel lines.

My Canadian girls contributed much to my happiness. The natural friendliness of the Jersey island folk made it easy for girls from overseas to settle down; and the Canadians soon became at home in the boarding house. They were the first of the influx of new boarders which was another encouraging feature of my term as Headmistress. On my arrival I found only twelve boarders. By the September term we had fifty and, by the following Easter, seventy. Before I left in the subsequent December, the boarding school was full.

This expansion meant a great deal of organising work. The first great advantage from this increase in numbers was that it made it possible to run separate boarding houses—one for senior, and one for junior pupils. This separation of seniors and juniors was good for everyone in view of the difficulties arising from the disparity in the ages of my pupils. These ranged from four and a half to nineteen. Under the new arrangement juniors had their meals at different times from the seniors and were carefully supervised by the matrons and trained nurses.

It also facilitated the organisation of the outside activities for the seniors and many of them were able to go to lectures, concerts and plays in the town. I am glad to say that many also elected to go to special services and missionary meetings and several to teach in Sunday schools. Nearly every one, boarders and day girls alike, helped at the Animal Welfare Fête. Some collected stamps which were sold for the Council of Justice to

73

Animals; others collected silver paper, the proceeds from the sale of which went towards supporting a crippled child. When suitable, boarders were allowed to see any worthwhile films.

The healthy increase in numbers to which I have referred was not, happily, confined to boarders. During the same period, day scholars increased by fifty to two hundred and eighty and I was doubly glad to see the friendships which sprang up between day girls and boarders. One such friendship, that between Mary and Agatha Dale-Harris and Marguerite Syvret, was enhanced by academic achievements. All three matriculated simultaneously.

I have already written of my friendship with the Dale-Harris family but not, I think, of that with Marguerite. This is a friendship not only of the past but happily of today—indeed I heard from her only the other day when she was answering an appeal from me to check some material I had for this book. I remember her always as an outstanding girl; she had curly, golden hair and lovely eyes. She has changed little and developed a great deal of personality. One has only to discuss anything with her to realise that, what with her clear brain and vivacious manner of speaking, she must be a thorough and interesting teacher. Her vivid, accurate descriptions and keen sense of humour capture one's attention. It is sheer joy to be with her. No wonder these other two clever Canadian girls, Mary and Agatha, found in her an inspiring friend.

Another lifelong friendship, begun at the school, was that between Agatha Dale-Harris and Moira Odlum. These friendships were one of the many things which Agatha tells me made her school days so happy in Jersey. What she found so wonderful, she says, was the feeling of complete freedom and the general atmosphere which seemed to foster the knowledge of how to enjoy community life. She recalls the Sunday evenings round the fire, and she could even remind me what books I read and the discussions we had about them. I was much in sympathy when she told me that she missed the peace when she came on to Westonbirt, for there the school had a 'gamey' spirit. I never can see why those who don't care for games should be pressed

74

to play. I'm sure this is usually pointless and for the P.T. staff to press their enthusiasm so much is anything but sporting.

Most of these friendships too seem to have lasted. Only the other day Susanne Coke, another happy student, came to visit me. She was on a visit from Toronto, and wanted news of Miss Holt, Miss Beechcraft and many others of the staff. She told me she had been in touch in Ireland with Denise Le Gallais and brought me news of all the other Canadians. It appears she has kept in touch with the group and, although it is now thirty-five years since we left Jersey, they are all as united as ever.

Perhaps because there were students from so many parts of the world, it was easy for all of us to maintain this wholesome breadth of outlook. And there was no doubt about our universality. In 1931 there were ten girls from Canada, two from Australia, one from Nassau, one from Austria and one from France. Besides these, there were many girls whose parents were still serving in India, Kenya, South Africa and the Near and Far East, all of whom, weaned in foreign ways, had idiosyncrasies of upbringing and outlook which had to be understood and lived with, just as they had to adapt themselves to our ways. Amongst these was Dorothy Chapman, another outstanding person, whose father was Principal of a college in China. Later she came to Cheltenham and is now enjoying a distinguished medical career in England.

The academic side advanced steadily. In 1932 Claire Oslear and Mary Dale-Harris went up to Westfield College, London, to read Classics. They were followed the next year by Marguerite Syvret and the year after by Lucy Foulerton and Pamela Bacon. Of these, four were Open Exhibitioners and the fifth became President of the Westfield College Union. Other girls achieved other types of distinction. One outstanding one is Doris Leach. She won the Jersey championship for diving and later became British Champion. Ever artistic as well as athletic she is now, I believe, devoting herself to pottery.

What happy memories! I realise how very fortunate I was to go to a place where I found so many friends. I cannot close this

Jersey chapter without mention of one or two others. There is Mrs. Le Maistre, for instance, who used to visit me at Westonbirt when her grandchild, Pamela Graham, was there; the Underhills; and Sir Sydney and Lady King-Farlow and their daughter, Cynthia, who later sent her clever daughter, Sally, to me at Cheltenham. There was Sir James Knott who, at his own expense, laid out the grounds and gardens of the college—and how beautiful they were. Then, of course, Sir Jesse Boot, who became Lord Trent in 1930 and Lady Trent. It was in Queen Street in St. Helier that he and Lady Trent had started their joint venture of Cash Chemists, incorporating a library. It was Lady Trent who looked after the library side in Jersey whilst her husband developed the pharmaceutical business, and although, later, the concern which they developed into such a vast business had its headquarters in Nottingham, he never lost his interest in or love for the island. One of his memorable works was the rebuilding of St. Matthew's Church into which he had installed the most exquisite Lalique glass windows.

With all the exciting but exacting activities of the college crowding upon me, it will be clear that there was not much time to indulge my passion for travel and seeing new places. Nevertheless Mary, Agatha and I managed to fit in a trip to Italy during Easter 1931. It was not an unqualified success, for, just as we were approaching Cannes and fortunately resting for a time, at 7 a.m. on Good Friday morning, a drunken, reckless driver—and the latter abounded in France—crashed into our car. He damaged it so badly that we could get no further than Cannes. Again, however, my luck held. At that time one of my uncles was chaplain there and Lady Trent was in residence. This saved the situation.

My only other journey, in the summer of the same year, was with Jessie Dykes who had come over from Canada. We drove to Oberammergau. Some of the journey and even the play itself was spoiled by bad weather, as also was Munich. We had ample compensation, however, enjoying the glories of the Châteaux Country on our return journey.

When the time came to leave Jersey, in December of 1931, all the great happiness I had known there filled my heart and I was truly sad to leave. I was nonetheless glad to be back in England, although I wondered what new problems would confront me at Westonbirt.

I appreciated greatly my successor, Miss Barton's reference in her report to my short period. She said, 'I want to express, though I know it has been done before, the gratitude which the school feels for the work done by my predecessor, Miss Popham. Though she was only in Jersey for five terms, she accomplished as much in that time as most people do in five years, and the school is reaping the benefit.'

WESTONBIRT

CHAPTER SIX

WESTONBIRT SCHOOL

∞∞∞

As I HAVE remarked previously, my desire to 'follow the star' invariably guided my decisions. However, on the occasion of my change from Jersey to Westonbirt, I also had the intervention of a crystal-gazer. She made her prediction early in November 1931 and even those who are sceptical about the gift of foresight must admit that this was fulfilled with quite startling accuracy. It was as I was driving along the sea front from St. Helier on my way to tea with friends in St. Aubin's, that I passed the house of Mr. and Mrs. Underhill. Mrs. Underhill and I had met at a party soon after they had come from India to settle in Jersey. We were at once drawn to each other in a curious sort of way; from that time onwards we had met frequently and Mr. Underhill came on to my staff as mathematics master in which capacity he was to prove a tower of strength. Percy (which was Mrs. Underhill's name) was a gay person; well read, full of ideas and conversation in the course of which we had often talked about India. She told me that during their stay there she had often been able to foresee happenings that occurred later.

On this particular afternoon she called to me from her garden where she was out pruning the roses.

'Do call in on your way back,' she shouted across to me, 'I have something to tell you.'

When I dropped in later in the afternoon she revealed her information:

'This morning when I was dusting my crystal I was thinking

79

of nothing in particular, when suddenly I became aware that you are going to leave the island before Christmas. I saw clearly that you are going to live for exactly five years in a huge square house with enormous and lovely gardens. Then you will make a move to an even larger grey building in the middle of a town.'

I could only greet this pronouncement with scepticism. Not in any way because I doubted her visions—she was essentially a person whom I trusted. But this particular prediction seemed quite beyond the bounds of practicability.

'I don't see how all this can possibly happen,' I exclaimed. 'I have to give a term's notice before I leave my present job. I am sure the Council would give me the same if they wanted to remove me.'

However, she was soon to be proved right. For only a few days after this I received a phone message from the Council in England asking me to come over at once.

On my enquiry as to the reason for this I was told: 'We want to talk to you about Westonbirt.'

'I know nothing about Westonbirt and care less!' I exclaimed. I can't remember to whom I was talking at the time but it was probably Mr. Warrington.

'Anyway,' he ended our conversation, playing his trump card, 'the Council has always done what you wanted and this is their first request to you.'

This was only too true and I crossed by the first boat.

When I met the Council they startled me with the proposition that I should move at Christmas from Jersey to Westonbirt. When I asked that, at least, I might go and pay a visit to the school with a view to seeing it before I made any decisions, I was blankly told that I should not be welcome there. All I gathered from my interview was that Mrs. Craufurd, who had been Principal for three and a half years—ever since the school had first opened in 1928, in fact—was leaving at the end of the term and that it would be quite in order for me to meet her after that. It appeared that at the moment she and her Principal

Assistant, Miss Mason, who was in charge of the academic side of the school, were not in agreement with each other.

I pointed out that, if all the stories one heard about Westonbirt being an aristocratic sort of place for the daughters of the rich were true, then surely I as merely a parson's daughter was not the person that they needed. I had been used to all sorts and conditions of people and I did not want to run a school just for a limited section of the community. I was a professional teacher and my chief concern was for the standard of the work.

At this stage Dr. Norwood intervened to say that this was precisely why they wanted me to go there. Westonbirt was a very young school and in his view it was essential that it be brought up to the sound educational standards of a really good public school.

'If you want to do a really good job for education,' he added, 'this is where you should go.'

Naturally this was an appeal which I could not resist.

I was sorry to leave all my Jersey friends but, as Percy Underhill had foreseen, I went to the square house with its lovely gardens and was there for exactly five years. At least, it was good to be back on the mainland rather than being tucked away on an island. I should perhaps explain that Jersey was much more isolated then than it is now. When I wanted to go to England during my time there I found the easiest way was to go by the potato or tomato boats which went direct to Weymouth, until one of my acquaintances who had a small private plane took me over several times. He always warned me it was a risk and that was only too true for, alas, soon after I left the island I heard the news of his death as a result of a crash into the sea.

Later on, I was very grateful for Dr. Norwood's advice and I now look back with amusement as I remember saying that I hoped that after five years I might then take over some quite small school!

When, rather sadly, I left Jersey at the end of the autumn term, I sent my possessions on to Westonbirt, and taking my car with me I went with Jester and Mickey to stay with Nora Almond at the Clergy Daughters' School at Bristol for Christmas. And a very happy Christmas it was.

On Boxing Day, however, my initiation to Westonbirt started. As I had been requested to, I rang up the housekeeper to say that I would arrive by car next morning. And what a morning! The gales and rain seemed to intensify visibly the further I penetrated into the country. The pictures of Westonbirt which I had seen had shown what looked like one of 'The Stately Homes of England', but it had not occurred to me that England's stately homes were in such isolated places as this, and as far as I was concerned this was by no means a draw.

Until it had been bought for the School, the house at Westonbirt, deep in the Gloucestershire countryside, had been the home of the Holford family, whose fortunes had been founded by Sir Richard Holford, Master in Chancery in 1693. The last owner of the house had been Sir George Holford and, as he had had no heir, at his death in 1926 the property had passed to Lord Morley, son of his sister, Margaret, who had married the third Earl Morley, famous for his services to Queen Victoria as Secretary of State for War. As this family had their own estate at Saltram at Plympton in Devon, they decided to sell Westonbirt House with its gardens and 550 acres of park and this is how Westonbirt School came into being in 1928.

When at last I reached the gates at the end of the long drive up to the house on that tempestuous December day, it seemed very remote indeed from the outside world. Apart from the church in the garden—it is quite the usual thing in the Gloucestershire villages for a church to be in a private park— and the small hamlet, Westonbirt was surrounded for miles on every side by fields and copses of trees. I know that the beauties of the Gloucestershire landscape rate highly, but I have my limitations as a lover of the countryside and I have to confess that this remote situation preyed on my nerves. The outstanding feature of the park was the long line of trees that bordered the end of the fields beyond the garden, so limiting the view and I developed an almost pathological hatred of these trees, always so static and immovable! I positively longed for the time when perhaps one or more of them would be blown down and thus give some variation to this monotony. In fact, during my time at Westonbirt I often felt so isolated that, when there was not time to go the thirty-seven miles to Cheltenham or the twenty odd miles to Bath, I would drive to the nearer smaller places, either Tetbury, Malmesbury or Stroud, just in order to see ordinary people walking up and down the streets.

However, on that first arrival on the day after Boxing Day I held my head high and, after dashing through the torrents of rain, I arrived at the porch of the huge front door. I had been asked by the housekeeper in the course of our phone conversation to go to the 'Yeoman's Entrance', but I had no clue as to which this was and in any case I felt that the main entrance was the proper place for me. Accordingly the dogs and I landed ourselves in the porch and I rang the bell.

Following much drawing of bolts and clattering of keys the door opened and I was received by a kindly person who informed me that he was Evans the butler. He had been in service with Sir George Holford and had been so devoted to the place that he had stayed on; and was to continue to do so both during my own five years and for many years after my time. What a blessing he proved to be!

Evans' welcome had been most pleasant and respectful; not so however that of the Housekeeper. If the comic side of the situation had not struck me so forcibly, she might indeed have made me regret my change of school. She was a tallish, grey-haired woman and the door had hardly opened when out she appeared and, with a clatter of badly fitting dentures, snapped at me:

'I am the Lady Superintendent, and the Lady Superintendent at Westonbirt is on the same footin' as the Headmistress.'

Ignoring this remark, but making certain very positive resolutions regarding the future, I proceeded into the hall, with its vast, marble pillars and flamboyant architecture, and asked to see my rooms. These proved to be spacious apartments, and, while I took stock of them, Evans arrived with my cases. Eventually I was shown over the whole house. It was a gloomy tour, as the place was deserted except in the kitchen for a chef with a crooked face wearing the white cap of his calling. As I went round, remembering the prediction of my crystal-gazer in Jersey, it was curious to note that the building was very large and square! . . . Adjacent to it was a courtyard surrounded by what had been stables, cleverly turned into classrooms with boarding house above, and a garden of such taste and beauty that one wondered how the same person who had laid it out could have lived with the silk tapestries, gilded walls and ornate, painted ceilings of the house.

I began to settle myself into my new quarters. Then the rain ceased for a spell and I was able to take Jester and Mickey out into the garden for a walk and discover the lily pond and church. Before turning in for the night, however, I was due for one more cheering and encouraging remark from *the lady superintendent*. Thankful to be alone with my dogs and on the way to bed and sleep, I was suddenly disturbed with a rude bang on the door and the housekeeper bounced in.

'Don't be surprised,' she said, not without an acid note of pleasure in her voice, 'if you get blown up in the middle of the night. Your bedroom is over the boiler-house and it could easily explode. Also, the ghost of Sir George frequently walks the gallery above.'

With the wind howling and moaning outside, the rain pelting down and beating a fiendish tattoo on the window-panes, and this last ghoulish warning ringing in my ears, I must admit to a feeling of depression and disenchantment at my welcome. I felt very much as if I had strayed into a Brontë novel! However, there was nothing to do but to reassure myself that I had tried to follow the star, and think of what Dr. Norwood had said when I demurred about moving. 'If you want to do a good job —go! Westonbirt is a very young school and must grow up to have fine traditions and give a first-class education.'

Anyway, I am always excited about the future and the next morning I was cheered by the agreeable person of Mr. Godwin, the Bursar, who turned up and was most helpful to me in arranging my rooms. Mr. Warrington had let me choose the carpets and I had brought my furniture from Jersey. Amongst this were a lovely old tall-boy and a grandfather clock which the staff and girls had given me, and which I still have in my London flat. He told me something about the place and the school. Amongst other things he took me up the 'Bachelor's Turret' which we used later as part of the junior house; though it was to prove impossible to prevent the pigeons entering and laying eggs on the beds!

After I had thus familiarised myself with my surroundings, I spent the next few days taking the dogs out and trying to get my affairs into some sort of workable order.

Then, on 1st January, Miss Maud Kidney the Secretary arrived and life changed. We took to each other at once, and I felt immediately that I had not only a friend but a very competent person to help me. Now I would be able to get the true history of the beginnings of the school from someone who knew the staff and all about the different aspects of life there. Our friendship began from that very first meeting and we have remained friends ever since. When I left Westonbirt, after she had stayed with my successor, Miss Grubb, for a time, Maud Kidney joined me at Cheltenham and since my retirement we have shared a London flat.

Westonbirt was most fortunate in having as its rector Mr. Timins, who acted as our chaplain. I shall always think with affection of this kindly 'Hunting Parson'; of his humanity and humour and his readiness to give us all his friendship and advice. I can see him now as he rode to hounds or on his parish duties. How dignified he was—so good-looking and so kindly, beloved by all! He and I also had in common a love of dogs, and Jester and Mickey at once recognised a friend.

How dogs know those who love them! The first time Bishop Headlam, the Bishop of Gloucester, came to see me, having been asked to do so by Bishop Harmer (late of Rochester), we were both dreadfully shy. He said he could not stay long. Then in came the dogs. They went straight to him as he stood by the fire, fawning round his legs, obviously wanting to be friendly. He immediately sat down and took Mickey on his lap. Jester cuddled up to him and Small, a lady terrier, somehow managed to find a purchase round his shoulders. I was grateful to them for breaking the ice. He stayed to tea, came round the gardens and talked of many things from religion to flowers, and from that day I had a friend to trust and confide in all through my time at Westonbirt and Cheltenham.

In spite of his great learning and awe-inspiring manner, the Bishop never held himself aloof. When I was eventually appointed to Cheltenham, he invited me to spend a night in his Palace in the Close at Gloucester. I have no outstanding recollection of the Palace except that, for me, it had one eerie aspect. This was the long corridor from the visitor's room to the bathroom along which was a row of chests of ponderous proportions on which were stacked an interminable collection of detective stories. Such was the atmosphere they created with their lurid titles, that one expected anything to happen at any moment—one almost feared to look behind one in case gunmen, corpses or ghosts should appear. The Bishop was an avid reader of 'Whodunits', and, wherever he went, his host and hostess would try to supply the latest to be published.

Others one could never forget were dear Dr. Sedgewick and his partner, Dr. Braybrooke, our local practitioners. These two kindly and efficient men were responsible for the health of the school, and how well and truly did they live up to their brief. The girls were very fond of them—so much so as to honour them with pet names, which were respectively 'Poo' and 'Piglet'.

I must, however, turn back to the opening of my first term. My predecessor, Mrs. Houison Craufurd, had returned to London and I had hoped to learn much from a meeting with her. At her suggestion we met at the Hunt Club in Grosvenor Street. It was not a profitable meeting, for she told me so very little: but I could see why staff and parents had been attracted to her, for she had a strong personality. She was dressed in a beautiful fur coat and looked most dignified, and I had the impression that she thought a professional schoolmistress like myself a 'come-down' for Westonbirt! Still, I was glad to have met her that once, and also to get to know and like Miss Mason during my first term, before she left to be married.

When Miss Kidney and I had had a few days together, the staff arrived and, close on their heels, the girls and their parents. I suppose, looking back, I should have felt more daunted than I did.

I am glad to have this opportunity to contravert some of the more exaggerated legends that have clung round Westonbirt even up to the present day. Indeed I can personally witness that stories such as that every girl kept her own horse and had her own lady's maid are entirely without foundation. It is, just the same, not easy to interpret the Westonbirt of which I took charge in 1932 in terms of our own society thirty or more years later. The early 1930s was still the day and age when some parents of good families and other people with money did not in general want their girls to enter the professions. They thought of 'work' solely in terms of voluntary jobs and societies. They were satisfied for their girls to enter society and the marriage market with hunting and large house-parties as the principal way of employing their time. There were still some parents who failed to understand that their girls could benefit both themselves and the community by further education and taking degrees that would fit them for a professional life. For such parents—and they were, of course, only a proportion—Westonbirt had catered.

But times were changing and it was clearly the feeling of the Council that not only were the teaching qualities of an excellent staff of mistresses being frustrated, but they evidently felt that they themselves could take a more active part in the movement for reform and improvement that was sweeping the public schools at that time. It was this that led to my own appointment and Dr. Cyril Norwood's comment which I have already reported. It will be appreciated that there was a certain atmosphere of unsettlement about the school as I took over and I have not the least doubt that my own feelings of apprehension were shared both by those I had to teach and to whom I had to give guidance, and also by their parents. Canada and my time in Jersey, where the nearly empty boarding school after I took over, had all its hundred places filled in a year, had taught me that the only thing to do was just 'to press on regardless' and keep on working for the best. We did not, on opening day, know whether a dozen or a hundred of those girls on provisional notice would leave at the end of the term, but it turned out to be the smaller number. So the few vacant places were easily filled.

The strength of Westonbirt was in its staff. I had a splendid team. With such teaching housemistresses as Miss Freeman, Miss Bevan and Miss Nora McErvel and full-time teachers such as Miss Joan Badock—Head of History, and Miss Potter the biologist, and Miss Gulland and Miss Medley, one could not go wrong. Again, there was Miss Lushington (now Mrs. Butler), who had been with me at Havergal and at Jersey College, who taught Classics. After the first term, she took over from me the house I had inherited from Mrs. Craufurd. My view is that the Head should know all the girls equally and therefore not be Housemistress of any one House.

Then there was Miss Dawson from Sherborne who had had one term with me in Jersey. Besides teaching art she took over Beaufort House and became housemistress for a term. She was followed in Beaufort House by Miss Gulland who taught English and shared much of the Scripture with me. With such a staff of inspiring teachers, it was not hard to build up the academic side and, in 1932, for the first time, girls went to Cambridge and London Universities.

My first task was to get to know the girls individually in order to make them realise the value of discipline and the joy of learning. Prayers on the first day had shown me that there was a lack of steadiness, for I observed that the more light-hearted ones

88

were talking behind their hymn books. Likewise, during break
on the first day some of the more lively ones collected in the
passage near my door and chanted repeatedly, 'We want
Mrs. Craufurd, we want Mrs. Craufurd'.

However, as I ignored them completely, this particular
gesture fell somewhat flat.

It did not take long with the backing of the staff to get the
spirit that I wanted; in fact, I sensed that most of the school was
very pleased to have a firmer discipline. I found that from time
to time a parent would enter a girl for the school and come to
see me with the remark, 'I don't really mind anything, provided
that she is happy.' I would always then try to make them see
that happiness is a by-product of other things. If girls are cared
for as to their physical well-being and properly fed in addition,
then in a good school they will learn to enjoy their work, their
leisure and their friends. In this way, quite unconsciously, they
become happy human beings. Happiness is the natural state of
a well-adjusted young person; many of the young people of
today would be far happier, better and more useful adults if
they had had more discipline and higher ideals given them in
their childhood, both at school and at home, and less indul-
gence. To me, school is a place where girls should adapt themselves to acquire knowledge and learn how to work and discover
the happiness of work well done. In the long run, work well
done is the leaven of life.

An essential adjunct to all this is a good library in which
young people as they broaden their minds can browse in their
spare time and develop their own widening interests. While, for
the more scholarly older girls, a good school library can give
inspiration for life.

We had all this at Westonbirt and in addition the advantage
of natural surroundings. In summer the girls spent a great deal
of their time in our spacious garden. One would see groups of
red cloaks spread on the grass as they studied or pursued their
own particular reading interests. Mrs. Craufurd had chosen a
becoming uniform in red and grey, so that the cloaks which I

added blended well with the remainder of the dress and were both attractive and immensely useful. Then, in addition to the garden, we had the occasional delight of a visit to Mr. Alexander's glorious orchid houses. Though whether or not the advantages of living in the country and seeing the remarkable *arboretum* outweighed those of a school where girls are more in contact with the life of a town where they can meet all different varieties of people, is an arguable point. Anyway, the girls at Westonbirt always seemed to me happy, contented and *alive*, and that is surely as it should be.

Then too I had to give my attention to the recreational side. I fear that I lost a measure of popularity with a section of my pupils when I declared that they could no longer go to the Hunt twice a week but on Saturday only. This was, of course, the only reasonable action for me to take in order to maintain a proper rhythm of work throughout the week.

It was a matter of personal regret to me that team games played such an important part in the life of the school. I have never been keen on girls playing nothing but team games, because although these may be beneficial in providing fresh air and exercise, it seems to me that the important thing is for girls to be allowed to use their own initiative in their leisure time. This was the attitude I took both at Westonbirt and subsequently at Cheltenham. The girls who had come on to me at Westonbirt, both from Jersey and Havergal and who had been more used to my individualist way of running things, confessed to me long after this that they had not enjoyed Westonbirt as much as the other schools, solely because of compulsory team games. They loved the staff and the rest of the life, but felt that the games were a bore. At Cheltenham in particular there were a few girls who were clever enough to escape such games altogether—they would go out for walks or bicycle in small groups, go out sketching or hunting for flowers. They were none the worse pupils or citizens for that, for surely it is better for a young person's development for her to enjoy what she is doing rather than unwillingly to play compulsory games.

Swimming I regard as important. Not only is it probably the finest form of exercise inasmuch as almost every muscle is used and likewise, except for high diving, it entails no shock to the body, but it should be an essential attainment for every human being from the point of view of self-preservation.

Then at Westonbirt the girls were fortunate in that their riding instructor, Mrs. Archer-Houblon, was not only such a splendid horsewoman that she later rode the Queen's horses and deputised for her at the practices for ceremonial occasions, but she was also an outstanding human being. The girls not only learnt the proper standard of riding from her, but also the standards required for life itself. When, to our great regret, she left us she was followed in the most proficient fashion by Gabriel Caffin, one of the old girls whom she had trained. Thus, with riding for those who could afford it, swimming in the summer term and a certain amount of golf available also, the recreational side of school life became more balanced.

As, after the first few months, the initial anxieties and apprehensions connected with the change of headship sorted themselves out, I was able to look around me and think of further developments.

In view of the many applications that I started to receive for girls under the normal school age to become pupils, we decided that we should do something about this and we opened one wing of the house for a number of girls under eleven. Someone coined the name of 'Bunny House' for this establishment and it was to prove a great success, especially when Elizabeth Wills-Browne came to take it over. She had been at Havergal, also in Gibraltar for a time, and brought fresh ideas. She had a great capacity for giving the young a free but disciplined life with a good foundation for their work in the higher forms. Later she came on to Cheltenham with me to take charge of the Junior Boarding House.

An incident in connection with the Bunny House which I remember vividly was the first visit of Mrs. Erica Frith, a Canadian. Having heard so much about me in Canada, as she wanted to leave her children in England prior to going to join her English husband who was a colonel serving in India, she had decided to come and see me at Westonbirt straight away, instead of looking round any other schools. One of the children was a boy, and of course we did not profess to take boys. Adrian, however, was too young yet to go to his preparatory school and I closed a blind eye. These two children were so small that at school prayers they would gradually slide forward until they disappeared from sight under the grand piano. Virginia, who looked as innocent as an angel, was, on the contrary, quite a monkey but she was also very clever. She was to do splendidly; later, at Cheltenham, she was head of her house and senior prefect of the College. She went on to read Classics at Cambridge and afterwards taught in two public schools. Eventually she married a district commissioner and, in spite of having had five children, she not only taught in the Teachers' College in Gambia, but also produced a syllabus and book for the college. Since her first visit Erica Frith has always remained a special friend. During the war she helped in various house posts in Cheltenham, and even now we keep in close contact.

My next thought was to open a Domestic Science House, in order to give further education to girls who had passed their School Certificate examinations and now needed training in the more practical subjects which would be useful to them in later life. In any girls' school there is always a group who develop better on these lines than they would with a purely academic course. The school houses were all full and accordingly for this fresh project I had to use one of the houses in the park.

Another amenity which I started was the school shop. This began with a bank balance of £8, but gradually its finances developed and it became an important adjunct to our efficiency and convenience thanks to the able management of Gladys Poignand, whom I have mentioned previously in my Havergal chapter, and who subsequently came on with me to Jersey and so to Westonbirt. She was a clever and lively teacher of French

and was always willing to dedicate her spare time to any activity
—fitting herself in the most dedicated fashion to the pattern of
life in the school.

Also we had a group of greenhouses converted into an art
studio where, under the guidance of Miss Stenning and then
Miss Insol, the girls turned out some excellent work. I am sure
that art can play an important part in a girl's development
and that quite often a good teacher will develop in them a
talent of which they have previously been unaware. Being
myself tone-deaf to the extent that I have difficulty in dis-
tinguishing one tune from the other—I even have to listen
carefully for the National Anthem!—I have always appointed
the best possible staff who could take their own initiative. I feel
that I did a good service to Westonbirt when I lured John
Somers Cox (now Lord Somers) and his delightful wife,
Barbara, to live in the village so that he could be organist both
in the school and at the church, as well as doing some teaching.

In regard to my own teaching I continued at first to teach
Latin and Greek, but then Miss Lushington and later Miss
Biddle took over from me as I wanted to devote all my time to
teaching Scripture, which gave me a closer knowledge of the
standard of intelligence of most of the girls at the school. One
drawback to being a Head is that one has to sacrifice so much
of the teaching that one loves and to turn one's mind to cares
of administration.

Time passed so quickly that our first Speech Day was on us
in no time. Dr. Alington, Headmaster of Eton, was our guest of
honour. The Council, with Lord Guisborough as Chairman,
Canon Foster Pegg and, of course, Mr. Warrington, turned up
in full force. I was particularly delighted to have two of their
members there in the shape of Mrs. Frances Abel-Smith and
Lady Fraser, both of whom were not only members of the
Council, full of help and ideas, but also good and lasting friends.
The Duchess of Beaufort, our close neighbour at Badminton,
who from its inception had taken interest in the school, invariably held pride of place on Speech Days and I found her a

charming and most helpful friend both at Westonbirt and afterwards at Cheltenham. Dr. Alington gave a fascinating talk on
being 'Open-eyed and open-minded'. He urged the girls to
realise that, even if to them some subjects seemed dull, if they
took on their task with eagerness they could always gain
something of value for life.

Another red-letter day of our first summer was the Old Girls'
Day in June. It brought some fifty old girls back to the school,
some of whom such as Elinor Poynton and Olga McDonald
became and remained my friends. That summer, too, we started
our practice of presenting a play in the garden. This particular
year it was Drinkwater's version of *The Pied Piper of Hamelin*.
Plays were to add greatly to the girls' joy of life and enrich their
interest in literature and the drama in particular. A number of
them, such as Tita Theotoky, wrote their own plays during the
winter season and even went on to cast them themselves.
Ultimately our dramatic activities were to lead us to considerable honour.

They were a great thrill to everyone in the school from the
youngest members to the most senior member of 'The Parlour'
as our prefects were called. (I do not know how this curious
piece of terminology came about, but it was coined in the early
days of the school.) At any rate our prefects were invariably
referred to as 'The Parlour' and had great influence as they
became more and more responsible members of the school.
Amongst their many responsibilities—and not the least—was
that of the production and editing of the school *Magazine*. In
1932, D. Kettlewell, now known for her art work—especially
stained glass, and Felicity Farquharson, later senior air hostess
of B.O.A.C., were joint editors. Two years later Barbara Forbes-
Adam and Rosemary Meynell took over, the latter of whom has
subsequently become a journalist of distinction.

I endeavoured to introduce my ideals of individual development into the girls' mental recreation also. In our remote fast-
ness in the country we were denied the amenities of concerts,
plays and cinemas, and I could see that my only recourse would

be to bring distinguished people to the school to give talks and lectures. I am quite astonished, as I look back, at the number of great men and women who honoured Westonbirt in this way.

We had as a matter of regularity each year our distinguished guests of honour on the annual Speech Day. I have already mentioned Dr. Alington and there were also Miss Maude Royden, Sir Alexander Godley, Dr. Cyril Norwood and Sir Arnold Wilson, M.P. He, as I recollect, coincided as our speaker with my final year at the school and I remember him not only for that reason, but also on account of his heroic death only a year or two later, when, having volunteered at the age of fifty-two as a rear-gunner in the R.A.F. Bomber Command following an accusation in the House that he was too sympathetic to the Nazis, he was shot down in a raid over Germany. Others of our invited speakers were John Masefield, the Poet Laureate; the poet Lawrence Housman; the Duchess of Atholl; Sir Edward Grigg, Head of the War Office; Hugh Walpole and E. M. Forster, the novelists; Mrs. Stanley Baldwin; Sir Ian Fraser, M.P.; and many others—all of whom spoke on their own special subjects, thus covering a vast field of knowledge and experience in a manner that the girls enjoyed immensely.

One lecture, which I personally found absolutely satisfying, was on 'Poise' by Diana Watt. With brilliant enlightenment, yet absorbing entertainment, she demonstrated the various exotic movements from which she had evolved her famous course of exercises. Our admiration was unbounded when we watched her—she was then aged seventy—balance herself on a huge golden ball and shoot an arrow into a panel on the staircase without losing her balance, or spoiling her perfect poise!

It was my third year at Westonbirt in 1934 that I particularly remember.

First of all, it was that year when a new body with Dr. Cyril Norwood as Chairman of the Council took over all the Trust Schools and organised the entire group as The Allied Schools. With this move there came an era of changes and improvements of which I was only too happy to take advantage. A much-needed covered way was erected from the main building to Beaufort House and the classrooms. This was to be a boon in all seasons, as it eliminated the tiresome need for the perpetual donning of raincoats and wellington boots just to get from one part of the building to another. Then, too, they sanctioned an improvement of the golf course, so that from then on we had a passable nine-hole course on which the girls were able to get in some serious practice.

It was in 1934 also that I conceived the idea of what was to be the first Citizenship House. I had in mind the many girls from Westonbirt and other schools who, after a season in London, had then no definite purpose in life. Their parents did not want them to take up a profession, but they still had a desire to be of service, and in those days they needed help to find the right niche. This was, of course, long before the day of the competing propaganda of our various Welfare State Ministries with their inducements for girls to enter as trainees in our modern social services. I am glad that I was able to pioneer this field on a more individual basis.

Accordingly, with the help of Mrs. Clive Neville-Rolfe, Lady Davson and other advisers, I began to work out a course for these older girls between the ages of eighteen and twenty-one, who needed help in this way. We fortunately had a house near the gates of the park and a little distance from the school where we could start a small boarding establishment for this purpose, which recruited its pupils from a variety of schools, and likewise a number of older women from the surrounding district who wished to take advantage of it.

Our course had to be a broad one such as to make each student realise that, before she could be of genuine service, she must be properly equipped for the challenge of life. She must have the opportunity of studying the world around her and of investigating the various branches of public work and service; and be in the position to assess her own capacity. The course, accordingly, included a study of the structure of national and local government, together with the geography and history of the Empire and Commonwealth, psychology, First Aid, home nursing, child care and modern languages.

It was by the greatest good fortune that Miss Margaret Godley came to see me while I was making my preparations for this venture. With her Oxford degree in Modern Languages, her vast experience in Egypt and her travels in India and many parts of the world, she was the ideal person to run the Citizenship House, and her appointment was a great success.

As I have explained, the majority of students lived in, while the older people from the district who joined the course came in daily. Thanks to the fact that the house itself was near one of the gates they were able to come and go freely without in any way disturbing the work of the school.

Such was the success of the house that on 4th June 1934, we were able to hold a Citizenship Week. We scheduled a series of fourteen lectures and these were followed by discussions divided into theoretical and practical. Dr. Woodward, Bishop of Bristol, opened the course and in his address he pointed out the need for a sincere and active Christianity which could combat the rising power of Communism and Fascism; and how our course was contributing to this splendid object. This stimulating week and the work of the House in general not only benefited 'The Citizens', but also its influence was absorbed into the school to the considerable benefit of all. Its initial success must be attributed to Miss Godley and the continuation of this to her successor, Miss Lister.

I am glad to think that it was the inspiration of other Citizenship Houses which followed. Margaret Godley had great gifts and, though I was sorry to lose her, I was glad that she went on to build up one of her own in London. This, too, was a great success, but after a time she left it in the hands of Dorothy Neville-Rolfe, whilst she herself went to work with Lady Wavell in India. After her return, while Dorothy moved to Ashridge, Margaret built up a splendid course in London with her friend, Edith Wood. This 'Look and Learn' still continues both in

London and in the lovely Idbury Manor on the border of Gloucestershire and Oxfordshire, which they established for boarders.

Later on I started a similar Citizenship Course at Cheltenham and others have started in other schools, so that our work at Westonbirt had a far-reaching effect with the work altering to fit the needs of the day, with each generation.

As I look back through the old copies of the Westonbirt *Magazine*, it is rewarding to observe how the list of successful School Certificate candidates lengthened and the number of academic distinctions increased during my five years' Headship. I can fairly claim that each year education was widening and deepening and our standards were being raised. Mary Maples won a prize for the best Scripture paper in England in the School Certificate exams, Cicely Hornby gained the British-Italian League prize in 1936 which earned her a three months' summer course at Perugia University and a special certificate, while many pupils gained the Prix du Grand Concours and their Certificates.

By 1934 Mary Dale-Harris was a classicist at Westfield in her third year, Agatha was reading Classics at Lady Margaret Hall, whilst Tita Theotoky was taking Modern Greats at Somerville; Felicity Farquharson was at Kings College, London, with J. Phillips; Pauline Armstrong was studying medicine at the Royal Free Hospital, London; Jennifer Skinner who, under the name of Jennifer Grey, made her name on the London stage, was by then at the Central School of Dramatic Art; J. Cox distinguished herself at the Bedford Physical Training College and Ruth Lyle at the School of Architecture in London. From this brief list, the names on which are but a small sample of those who went on to advanced work, it will be seen that the numbers of girls going on to university increased each year. Thus, by December 1936 I was able to hand over the school to Miss Grubb in full confidence that it was firmly set to give each individual a background of sound education and training for life in whatever activity she elected to pursue.

Westonbirt

I do not, however, think I should conclude this chapter on Westonbirt without mentioning a number of incidents which stand out amongst the crowded memories of my five years' stay.

It was on 1st July 1936 that there occurred the highlight of my years at the school when the Duchess of Beaufort not only invited me to dine during the time that she had the then Duke and Duchess of York—the late King George VI and the present Queen Mother—staying with her, but did the school the honour of asking our Dramatic Club to perform *Comus* (which she had seen acted on Speech Day) in the gardens of Badminton House for the royal guests. The contemporary report confirms that 'everything went with a wonderful swing and at the very end the principal actors were presented to Their Royal Highnesses'.

A further incident that comes to mind as perhaps a contrast to this one is when I allowed my humanitarian instincts and my feeling of compassion for animals to overcome my sense of social propriety. Although I enjoyed seeing the Hunt when the Duke held the meet in our own park and appreciated the beauty of the lovely horses and the splash of colour as the pink coats raced across the fields, I could never bring myself to think it right to breed foxes specially for hunting, even though it might be necessary to exterminate them to prevent them preying on the farms. Thus, one day, when the Hunt had found a scent across the park I happened to be in one of the classrooms on the ground floor of Beaufort House when the unfortunate hunted fox entered to find refuge from his pursuers. I had no hesitation about shutting him in the room to preserve him until the Hunt had passed through the grounds. I suppose that I would have suffered a heavy loss of status throughout the district had my friends of the Hunt ever discovered this, but I just cannot bear to think of animals being killed for pleasure! It is this same instinct that today prevents me, much as I love dogs, from keeping them in a London flat where they are unable to get sufficient freedom and exercise.

Then, of course, we had a number of incidents of real comedy, such as manifest themselves in any institution from time to time.

Boring—Never!

The funniest of these concerned the housekeeper whom I engaged early in 1932 to replace the 'Lady Superintendent' whom I have already mentioned in my story. The main feature of this lady was that she was so round and fat that the girls used to laugh at her efforts to squeeze into her Baby Austin, and say that she needed a shoehorn. She at first appeared a paragon of virtue who for some time served up a varied menu of considerable excellence. But, alas, this was not to last. After some time it became manifest that custard appeared on the menu with an almost intolerable frequency. Later, certain other brand foods arrived to keep the custard company and investigation soon revealed that she was collecting coupons on the custard and similar gifts from the others. Our confidence was not a little shaken. Then one day when I had been out I returned to find a very agitated Mr. Godwin. From his investigation in the Bursar's office, he revealed that our paragon had been engaged in a falsification of the wages sheets. When challenged she had tried to throw the relevant account sheet into the fire and, being so fat, she had toppled over in her agitated state, rolled on the floor and burst all her apron buttons. This must have been a comic sight, but the poor Bursar was in no mood for laughter and, of course, I had to interview her myself.

This distressing interview took place just outside my study door when she defended herself with spirit and vigour; at one stage she started throwing her arms in the air, while in dramatic tones quoting Kipling's 'If—'. Suddenly with a wide sweep of her flailing arms she knocked, with an almighty clatter, a table on which rested the brass stair rods which had been taken up for carpet cleaning. Instantly the door of my study was flung open and Miss Kidney and Mr. Godwin appeared looking white and scared. I think they feared that I was being murdered. Our poor fat lady had, of course, to go. But how we laughed at it all afterwards!

Then, too, the care of the girls was not always without its anxieties which appear more humorous in retrospect than they did at the time.

Westonbirt

There was our girl from Katmandu whose father had been in the Diplomatic Service in Nepal, during which time she had been used to a free and easy way of life that did not easily adapt itself to school routine. Joan arrived for the September term. She was a big girl for her age but terribly shy. One evening quite soon after her arrival she was absent from roll call. A search was immediately organised but it failed to relieve our anxiety. There seemed no trace of her. Thinking she might have tried to go home, I phoned her parents who were living in Surrey and at the same time notified the police. As may be understood, I was greatly worried and prayed fervently that I should soon hear that she was in touch with her parents, but by morning there was no sign. All the ground staff were sent out to search, amongst them being a funny old man who cheered us up with the remark: 'I thought I see'd a 'ead a'sticking out of a 'aystack,' which was not exactly encouraging. Eventually, later in the morning when I was beginning to get frantic and her anxious parents had appeared at the school, Joan reappeared quite unconcerned. It seemed that she had gone to sleep in the garden and wakened to realise that she was late for supper. Not being sure in the dark how to find her way back into the school, she went into the woods, rolled up in her cloak and slept until morning. My relief at this can well be imagined.

My final incident is one that I shall never forget. This was when I saw to my horror three girls climb out of a top-floor window and move slowly along a very narrow ledge towards the adjacent window. My heart stood still, but of course I dare not utter a warning for fear one of them should look down and lose her balance. In an agony of apprehension I watched the slow manoeuvre as, one by one, they shuffled along the ledge and climbed in to the next window. How thankful I was to see the last one safely home! I was so relieved that I could not be as severe with them as I should have been. However, I did not fail to make them realise the anxiety which their silly prank had caused.

* * * * *

Boring—Never!

It was at the end of 1936 that my five years at Westonbirt terminated in the manner which I shall have to describe in my next chapter. By this time, of course, there was already the apprehension of another war overhanging the world. We were perhaps, all of us, somewhat naïve to think that our efforts for promoting peace through the medium of the League of Nations were to be of avail against a vicious and unprincipled character such as had arisen in Germany in the shape of Adolf Hitler. I had seen something of the tension arising in Europe at first hand when in the summer of 1933 Maud Kidney and I went to visit the Masaryks in Czechoslovakia—it will be remembered that Olga, the daughter of President Masaryk, and I had been friends during my time at Westfield during the First World War. But our visit had another significance as well in the first-hand acquaintance we had of the rising fear of Germany in Central Europe. When, after staying with the Masaryks, we went to explore the Lower Tatras we had to carry an introductory note from the President with us to make certain that we could obtain hospitality at the inns. Otherwise there was the danger of our being suspected of being German and not being able to obtain accommodation for the night. Indeed, one had to open every conversation with the words, 'I am English.'

Looking back in retrospect I am glad too that I was able to make other trips before war once again encompassed us and put an end to such excursions. One of these was a visit to the Holy Land to stay with Margaret Nixon who was chief secretary to General Wauchope, High Commissioner in Jerusalem.

Then in summer 1935 I was able to pay a visit to see my old friends in Toronto. This was, unexpectedly, an occasion for anxiety inasmuch as I had had a letter from the Chairman of Havergal telling me that on Miss Wood's impending retirement I would be offered the Headship there. However, it was while I was still pondering on this that the further stage in my career unfolded itself in quite different fashion and the question of returning to Canada did not arise.

CHAPTER SEVEN

CHELTENHAM LADIES' COLLEGE—PRE-WAR

❖❖❖

IT WAS on a fine Sunday afternoon in May 1936 that my friends, Miss Schooley and Mrs. Parks, whom I knew in their capacity as His Majesty's Inspectors of Schools, rang me to suggest coming over to Westonbirt to see me. I readily said, 'Yes.' It was in the course of tea that the former mentioned that the Principalship of Cheltenham was vacant and expressed her curiosity as to whether I would be making an application.

This suggestion amused me greatly. 'Surely Cheltenham wouldn't think of me?' I exclaimed. 'Anyway, I really couldn't cope with a school of that size.' I concluded by saying that I knew very little about Cheltenham and had never even seen the College.

This did not surprise them for it is possible to visit Cheltenham and even live there for many years without noticing the College very much, even though this is right in the centre of the town. The Georgian houses and the tall trees that line the Promenade from St. George's Road up to the Queens Hotel obscure that part of Montpelier Street on which the main buildings are situated.

Needless to say, in the coming years, I was to become extremely familiar with these buildings. The main entrance is in the older part of the College on St. George's Road and it is little wonder that, amongst some of those who have had only the opportunity to judge us from external experiences, we have a somewhat monastic reputation. For that is the impression given by the granite walls and turretted bastions of this part of the façade. However, once through the tunnelled darkness of the entrance, the picture changes completely. My memories are of bright sunshine (of which the Cheltenham climate provides an unusually large share) and of green lawns neatly divided by paths and beds of gay flowers.

The rambling edifice which constitutes the College as it is today began with the group of buildings, mainly neo-Gothic in style, at the corner of Montpelier Street and St. George's Road. These have spread to take in the large quadrangle bordered by Montpelier Street on one side, Fauconberg Road, Bayshill Road and St. George's Road on the others. The principal extensions I should mention are the Princess Hall on Montpelier Street built in 1897 and the adjacent gymnasium which was opened thirty years later, in 1927. Then to the extreme west on Fauconberg Road there is the Cotswold House which, intended as the Principal's House, was completed at the time of my arrival in 1937. Again, along Bayshill Road to the north, there are the buildings which also were nearing completion at the time of my arrival and which in May 1937 were opened as our West Wing by Lady May Abel-Smith. This was a splendid occasion with the beautiful Cotswold stone showing to advantage in the summer sun, when we could all appreciate the extent to which these new buildings would be an asset to the appearance of our bright quadrangle of lawns.

But, to revert to the beginnings of my own association with Cheltenham, Mr. L. S. Wood, a well-known scholar to whose credit, I believe, lies part of the compilation of the Oxford Book of Quotations and who had also been one of His Majesty's Inspectors, came over from Cheltenham to see me the morning after the talk which I have mentioned. His opening conversational gambit was to the effect that he had heard that I had treated with undue levity the suggestion that I should apply for Cheltenham and, as one of the members of the Council of the College, he felt that he ought to warn me that there was a letter in the post to me from the Chairman, Lord Askwith, inviting me to apply and to go for an interview with the Council in London.

Surely enough the letter arrived in the following morning's post and, even before school hours had started, I was on the phone to Dr. Cyril Norwood, then Master of St. John's College, Oxford, arranging to drive over to see him for a talk that same afternoon.

I challenged him as to whether he was behind this move and, though I got no change out of this suggestion, I still suspect that he was one of those who had proposed me: Bishop Harmer, who had been on the Cheltenham Council at an earlier date, was, I think, another. The latter in particular had much influence at the Ladies' College inasmuch as Mrs. Harmer (*née* Somers-Cox) was at the college with Miss Beale and must have known her very well, for I remember her telling me how Miss Beale had one day asked her to accompany her to London to help choose a new bonnet! When she died she left me a few bits of china and a painting of the Madonna on wood which Miss Beale had given her. These I treasured greatly and I gave the china to the Guild when I retired, while the Madonna still hangs over my bed. Adeline, their daughter, whom I have already mentioned, was at Cheltenham under Miss Beale's successor, Miss Faithfull.

Miss Faithfull had also, it appeared, discussed me with some members of the Council, but she was also supporting another candidate. I am reasonably certain that she would not have given me any support at a later date when we came to know each other better. Although we remained friends and she often asked me to her thatched house on Birdlip Hill she would say to me, 'My dear, in *my* time, we . . .'; to which I was once rash enough to answer, 'Yes, but you retired in 1922 and these are the late 1930s; what was right then, might not be the best now.'

Anyway, once again, it seemed, it was a matter of my 'following the star'. So I sent in my application, not expecting for one moment that I should be appointed.

When I went for the interview, the two other short-listed candidates and I all had lunch with a number of the members of the Council. I was sitting next to Lord Askwith, with I think Mr. Weech on my right and, as it really didn't occur to me to behave differently from the way I did at any other lunch, we talked very happily. Afterwards one of the others said to me, 'You seemed very much at ease at lunch and having an animated conversation.' So I supposed at the time I had not done the right thing, but, not expecting to be appointed, I wasn't worried.

But when a little while later in the day I met the whole august body of the Council to a number of almost thirty, that was quite another matter. They asked me a great many questions, of which I don't remember a single one, except the final one, 'What are your hobbies?'

This last word gave me a fleeting vision of small girls with teddy bears or dolls and small boys with tin soldiers or trains.

My mind went blank and, hesitatingly, I said, 'Dogs.'

'Don't you ever read?' asked Lady Barlow caustically.

Then I left the room quite certain that no one would appoint me. When Colonel Tarrant, who had been Secretary to the Council from Miss Beale's time, came out later and asked me to return to the room and Lord Askwith told me that they had appointed me, I was so overcome with surprise and with awe at the responsibilities which I now faced that I forgot all else.

I had arranged to spend the night in Surrey with friends, Mr. and Mrs. Spencer. He was a member of the Westonbirt Council, and their daughter was at the school. I got into my car and made for my destination in such a state of agitation that when, as I drove through Kingston High Street, having missed my way, I heard the sound of gongs behind me, I merely went faster and faster until the police car eventually caught me up as I reached the by-pass. Here I received the ticket which I no doubt well deserved and a few days later was fined the sum of £1 by the Kingston Magistrate, Mr. Blake-Carne, whose daughter Barbara, so I later found out, was at Cheltenham. He was most amusing about it when he came to see me at the beginning of my first term.

Cheltenham—Pre-War

The news of both my appointment and my court conviction for speeding were announced in the papers simultaneously, to the amusement of many of my friends, who quite correctly guessed that one was the consequence of the other.

Little did I envisage on that day how utterly devoted I should be to Cheltenham and that I had sixteen years and two terms in front of me at a school to which during the whole of that time I should dedicate my entire energy and affection.

When I went first to visit College in the autumn of 1936 nothing could have been more different from the reception which I received on my first arrival at Westonbirt; Miss Janet Macfarlane, Vice-Principal and Acting-Principal owing to Miss Sparks' illness a few months before, had invited me to a formal tea party in the Princess Hall to meet the staff. Each member of this was introduced to me in turn, but for me the arrangements were rather confusing for, as the 130 or so staff arrived in line at the Princess Hall, the porter called out the name of the one at the door, just when Miss Macfarlane was introducing to me the member of the staff five places ahead.

This was doubly confusing! It was difficult enough in any case to absorb the names of so many at the same time. I do remember, however, my joy in finding amongst them A. K. Clarke, whom I had first met in 1919 at the Kent Classical Association and with whom, together with Evelyn Gedge, I had made particular friends at that time. Indeed, Amy Clarke and I had continued to have many mutual friends and it was a reassurance to me to know that there was so outstanding a classicist on the staff. Our friendship has been a deep one from that time onwards and still is. This tiny person with a brilliant brain, real scholarship, goodness and wisdom has been a mainstay throughout my life ever since. She is often kind enough to visit me here today at my flat in Kensington High Street and has at this time of writing been of help and comfort to me since I am unused to the toils and tribulations of the author's task.

There was also in this gathering Maude Winnington-Ingram, Scripture Mistress for years at the College. Her sister Ethel had taught me English in the sixth form at Blackheath High School, and to her I owe my love of the great poets. These two nieces of the former Bishop of London were inspiring teachers indeed.

Following this party I visited Cheltenham several times during the autumn before taking up my work in January 1937, as both Miss Macfarlane and Colonel Tarrant wanted me to see the new Principal's house to which I have already referred. This was a charming house built in Cotswold stone toning in with the new west wing of the College, whose design had originally been approved by Miss Sparks. I can't say that I ever grew to love it myself, for I felt that it was built too low and it did not get very much sun owing to the trees in Fauconberg Road. But I was lucky in that the Council was providing some of the furniture and this was in beautiful taste owing to the choice being in the hands of Elizabeth Philipson-Stow, who was a member of the Council for many years and also a truly brilliant Secretary of the Guild of Old Girls. Her contribution to College and the work of the Principal was inestimable. I am still immensely grateful for her help and friendship. As we both hold strong opinions we did not always agree, but to my mind the capacity to disagree over some points does much to strengthen friendship. I could count on her always to speak her mind truthfully and to give helpful criticism. This is friendship indeed.

Another member of the Council whose acquaintance I made before I arrived on the scene at Cheltenham was Violet Tinson and we were to remain friends up to the time of her death in 1959. The first time we met she took me for a long drive through the Cotswolds and over Cleeve Hill. It was a lovely day with the countryside of Gloucestershire glowing in the sun with the trees and autumn flowers in the gardens looking their best. I shared the exhilaration of these surroundings and I took the opportunity of expressing my appreciation of her kindness, as I was well aware that she had not voted for me at the time of my interview. I felt no ill-feeling about this, as it is my belief that every individual has the right to his or her own opinion and this

is why for so many years I have been an active member of the
Society for Individual Freedom. Anyway, I do think that my
frankness on this occasion cemented our friendship and led to
my eventual acquaintance and friendship with her sister, Rachel
Tylden, whom I also liked immensely. The Tyldens had lived
in South Africa until 1936 but on her return I often saw her and
Ray, her daughter, was in C.L.C. until she went on to read
Modern Languages at Cambridge. Rachel Tylden was a person
of many gifts and was most adaptable. Her activities included
such fascinating things as constructing an old village for the
Newbury Museum and she was, in fact, completing some work
for the Ashmolean at Oxford when she was suddenly taken ill
and died. Like Violet, she is missed by many.

I was also fortunate in my start at Cheltenham inasmuch as I
already knew General and Mrs. Peebles and their daughter,
Joanna, who lived there in a house with a particularly lovely
garden in the Park. Although I had not known it, General
Peebles was on the Council at the time of my appointment.
He stayed in London after the meeting and his wife later told
me that he had rung her up to say, 'The Pop is in.' He retired,
however, before I became Principal for he was elderly and not
in good health. But I continued my friendship with Mrs. Peebles
and Joanna after his death and when they went to live in
London.

I was delighted that Lady Fraser (known to her friends as
'Chips'), who had been a member of the Westonbirt Council,
agreed to be my representative now on the Council of C.L.C.
All the world knows her husband Ian Fraser (now Lord Fraser
of Lonsdale) who, though blinded in the First World War, for
so many years gave such splendid service as M.P. for the
Lonsdale division of Lancashire, and likewise as Chairman of
St. Dunstan's and Vice-President of the Royal National Institute for the Blind; as well as being Chairman of the British
Legion. We can all remember how he did not allow his dis-
ability to interfere in any way with the pursuit of a devoted
career in public life: and I remember him, in particular, when

he visited us and gave an inspiring lecture to the girls. The two of them always worked together and did so much to help those who had suffered similar misfortunes. Also they are such wise and gay people that everyone values their friendship.

It was eventually on 1st January 1937 that I settled into my new house and took up my duties as Principal of Cheltenham. The few days before the beginning of the term gave me the chance to get to know Mary Shaw, who was head of Lower College, and other senior members of the staff who had also come back to Cheltenham early. I was also able to make the acquaintance of the 'Houseladies' as the mistresses in charge of houses are called.

It was a terrifying procedure getting to know each member of the over hundred strong staff personally and then having the influx of so many girls to cope with. However, there was an indefinable something in the spirit of the College that captured me at once and fortified me. As I thought of all that I had read of Miss Beale and listened to Colonel Tarrant's tales of her times I felt very humble and unworthy. Colonel Tarrant had been everything to Miss Beale from office boy to trusted Bursar and Secretary to the Council. His whole life was one of devoted service from that time on until his retirement in 1945.

My worst moment was that of Opening Prayers on my first day. Visitors are always welcomed at College Prayers but, I suppose in order to see what the new Principal was like, so many turned up on this occasion that the enormous Princess Hall which holds at least 1,500 people was packed to the roof. I can't remember the theme of my talk, but I remember telling them of a cartoon I had seen depicting on one side crowds of wild animals, lions, tigers, elephants and other large animals, and on the other side a small wire-haired terrier, facing them terror-stricken and saying, 'If I wag, will you wag back?' I said that I felt at that moment like that terrier. This joke fortunately went down and how grateful I was to all those old Cheltonians, staff, parents and girls who responded to my approach so quickly and who have given to me their friendship and understanding.

It had somehow been symbolic for me that during my first
hours at Cheltenham I had recognised the College emblem of a
daisy with the motto 'COELESTI LUCE CRESCAT', for my
old Headmistress of Havergal, Miss Knox, was trained at
Cheltenham and had imported these to Canada, and it was
borne in on me how much Canada owed to Cheltenham Ladies
College. I mused how Miss Knox had founded Havergal and
had been its first Principal, so that even in my day there it was
still a growing school making tradition largely based on
Cheltenham. Jersey College for Girls with its numerous successive headmistresses had not really been able to build up a
long tradition, while even Westonbirt was only three and a half
years old when I went there. To what extent, I wondered, was
I with this background going to be in sympathy with a college
and guild so steeped in tradition as was Cheltenham? Yet it
was not long before I recognised in College the enormous value
of its tradition, and the power which came from it. The spirit
with which it was imbued provided me with inspiration. It had
been founded in 1853 and became a famous school under the
guidance of Miss Beale. She was one of those really great headmistresses with foresight and courage to overcome all obstacles
and whose aim was to build on a deeply spiritual basis with
service to country and humanity in the forefront of its ideals.

Miss Beale in particular had been a forward-looking person,
ahead of her own time in many ways. Thus it was borne in on
me that traditions and alterations in accordance with the needs
of changing times were not so much contradictory as com-
plementary: from the first I made up my mind that, if we were
to maintain the ideals that the College had stood for in the past,
we must move with the times and look to the future.

I was determined that I must modernise in such a way as to
send out into the world each generation of girls properly
equipped to give their best service to their fellow men and
women and that the details of school life must change, but not
the spirit. My first step was to change the uniform for all the
girls; black velour hats with wide hatbands were gradually

replaced by modern palish green felt hats, black stockings by brown ones and the navy tunics by green coats and skirts, so that in style of dress they would fit comfortably into the world of their own generation. Mrs. Carlisle of Bunwell House was my great aid in this respect and took over much responsibility for the clothes. Later, as Senior Housemistress, she relieved me of all the troublesome details and backed me in keeping a high standard of neatness which much encouraged the good deportment which I regarded as essential. A much-beloved Houselady, Jessie Carlisle remained in College from 1934 until her retirement in 1956, since when I am glad to say we have continued to keep in touch and I have stayed with her in her lovely old manor house, 'The Barns', at Greet, near Winchcombe.

One cannot pretend that one is able to make even such small changes as this without incurring a measure of criticism. Some people indeed—and they are to be found in all spheres of life—find it hard to distinguish between true tradition which can keep the same spirit but take different forms as it adapts itself to the different ways of each generation, and what can only be called a negative stick-in-the-mud attitude.

The new wing was used first for the Junior School, whilst Hatherley Court, a newly acquired house, with its lovely garden and space for tennis courts, gave the Junior Boarders an ideal home and provided much more ground for sport for the rest of the college. I was fortunate enough to obtain the services of Elizabeth Wills-Browne who had run the 'Bunny House' so happily at Westonbirt and she brought all her gifts of leadership for these young ones to the management of the Juniors at Hatherley, where she and Miss Hadfield and her spaniel Kelpie were in their element.

Here again romance enters my story for my Jester in his old age fell head over heels in love with Kelpie and was frequently missing on account of his urge to go off and visit her at every opportunity. I did not always have the time to go and retrieve him from his amorous adventures, but in some mysterious way he would manage to get home in one way or the other. It was by no means a rare thing to see a taxi draw up at my gate at the College, then out would get Jester while the kindly taxi-man drove on. I was naturally in a perpetual state of terror that he would be run over during the course of his wanderings, but he always turned up safely. Used to the spacious country life, he took to walking to the sanatorium on Leckhampton Hill by some cross-country route of his own. On one occasion a signalman from the Leckhampton signal box some two miles out of town, rang up to say that he had taken him in to give him refreshment as the poor dog seemed tired! It will be gathered that Jester was soon quite a well-known 'man about town' as far as Cheltenham was concerned.

To revert, however, from dogs and juniors to the more serious aspects of education, I had often wondered in my smaller schools how one would get to know each and every girl in a large school, so that one could help each one to have a life of her own in order to develop her own personality to the full. But after a very short time, I had convinced myself that the College can give more in every way just because of its size and the house system. I have absolutely no doubt about this.

The Houseladies were of inestimable help in this inasmuch as they knew their girls well and would keep in close touch with me over each individual girl, while I in turn visited the Houses frequently whether by invitation or merely dropping in in casual fashion. I soon found that in the house community of fifty to sixty girls in each house, the girls themselves made many lasting friendships and had the benefit of a real home life, with a training in manners and much preparation for practical and social life.

On the other hand the College itself was, in the true meaning of the word, able to give all pupils a 'comprehensive' education, with five or six parallel forms. This enabled the placing of each girl according to her ability, but with her own contemporaries. The extra sub-division of these parallel classes in Classics, Modern Languages and Mathematics meant that a linguistically able girl in C or D class would move to an A class for languages. Or vice versa so that one slow at Maths in an A class could join the B class in this subject, thus each girl could go rapidly ahead in subjects for which she showed ability, while, at the same time, progress slowly and surely in those where she had difficulty.

The size of the school, too, had many advantages in other ways. One could, for instance, invite distinguished people to speak knowing that they would be assured of having a worthwhile audience. Likewise, with such a large selection of talent to choose from, the College was able to make up its own orchestras and organise competitions between the Houses in singing, handiwork, deportment and various other accomplishments. This also applied to the numerous teams in games and swimming.

My first term, spring 1937, was like every other spring term, occupied with the preparation for Confirmation which always took place before Easter. Although I made a point of interviewing every candidate personally, I did not take Confirmation Classes myself that first year. I left this until the following year when candidates began their classes in the autumn.

Our preparation for this important event in a young person's life was taken extremely seriously, each girl attending one class a week from mid-October to Confirmation the following Easter, with myself or Miss Winnington-Ingram or Miss Sadlier and later Miss Grinling, and one with the rector or vicar of the church she attended. It became my custom to see each candidate every year and to impress on her the need to take her promises seriously, at the same time urging her that, if she was not ready to do so, she should postpone her Confirmation. I am sure that young people should receive Confirmation at the age when they are convinced and have a proper feeling of dedication towards it, which may well be at any age from eleven plus to eighteen or nineteen. Some people, I know, would place the minimum age even below eleven, as, of course, do the Roman Catholics. So much depends on the home background which may either be helpful or quite the opposite.

The spring term was also the term of the Entrance and Scholarship Examinations and this involved interviews with the parents of our prospective pupils. Then too we had 'Lent Lectures' given in my first year by Canon Maynard Smith of Gloucester and each year by some other distinguished person who had the capacity to put spiritual truths in intelligible language.

Ever since her visit to Westonbirt Dr. Maude Royden and I had kept in touch. Maude Royden was a remarkable person and long years before I met her I had heard her preach at her church in Orchard Street and I was conscious from listening to her that her religion penetrated the whole of her life of wide interest and travel. As an Old Cheltonian herself and a member of Guild she fulfilled her promise to give a lecture at Cheltenham in the summer of 1937. This was an unforgettable occasion, for she spoke of the need to develop mind and spirit and pressed the girls to enlarge their experience as much as possible by visiting all parts of the British Commonwealth. She urged everyone to remember the spiritual tradition of Britain and we must, she said, fulfil this by doing all in our power to assist nations to live in peace and freedom. It was in 1937 also that we had A. F. Tschiffely's lantern lecture on his rides throughout the countries of South and Central America from Buenos Aires right up to Washington, through heat and cold, rain and drought, over the Andes, down into the jungle and through Mexico which at the time of his visit was having one of its numerous revolutions of that era. We were all enchanted with his pictures of his two stalwart Argentine horses.

In contrast with the usual summer associations of Speech Days, I had inherited the custom at Cheltenham of a Speech Day in November, and in 1937 I can well remember this under the chairmanship of Lord Askwith with Earl Baldwin as our visiting speaker. (It was naturally some disappointment to us that while, when we had invited him earlier in the year, he was still Prime Minister, he had retired in the June of that year, and was now living privately at his home at Astley Park,

Worcestershire.) In 1938 he was followed by The Right Hon. Leslie Burgin, Minister of Supply. From 1939 onwards I changed the routine and put Speech Day into the summer term when we could enjoy its more customary associations of summer weather and the gaiety of our gardens. I came to the conclusion that it would be better for us to have only one big function a year, and accordingly I decided to alternate Speech Day with the Guild Biennial Meeting.

An interesting incident during my first year had been a visit from Emperor Haile Selassie, then living in Bath as an exile during the Italian occupation of his country. He wished to enter his eldest daughter. When I received his letter I rang up the Duchess of Beaufort to ask her advice on the proper beginning and endings for my letter in reply. For I will never be 'the obedient servant' of any except my God and my King or Queen as the case may be! She agreed with my sentiments and told me to write to 'His Majesty' and end 'Yours sincerely'.

I did this, and as a consequence, this charming man accompanied by one of his sons came over to see the College and I took him around. He was interested in everything, but insisted on my speaking French. Whilst I understand this language perfectly, I had really forgotten how to speak! However, we got on very happily and then also Miss Macfarlane came to the rescue. When he told me that his daughter was twenty-one and had already done her nurse's training at St. Thomas's Hospital, the situation became embarrassing. I begged him not to send her on the grounds that, being so much older than the other girls, she was unlikely to be happy.

He still wanted to see the Senior House, so I took him to St. Hilda's, the only senior house then. Here Miss Baron, the warden, was even more tongue-tied than I was, but fortunately there was a girl who spoke fluent French which impressed him and made him even more keen to enter his daughter. I'm sure the daughter would have been charming, but I had to ask myself could she have fitted in with all the younger girls after so much freedom? Anyway, the question was finally settled when he asked if we had other foreign girls. I said, 'Yes, a great many,' and mentioned, amongst them, one Italian and one half-Italian. In the light of his crucial situation with that country that decided him against the venture.

Only two years ago a friend of mine who lives for the most part in Ethiopia asked me to go and work there, and I, remembering this very gracious Emperor, longed to accept her invitation, but it was not possible for me to go.

Then only recently I saw him on television. He did not appear to have changed at all during the intervening thirty years since I met him at Cheltenham. Little wonder that, at the time of our first meeting, I thought of him as old, but he must, of course, have been quite a young man in his early forties.

Also in 1937 the Duke of Bedford, grandfather of the present Duke, founded for the College the 'Duchess of Bedford Scholarship', which is awarded to a pupil going on from the College to take up surgery. It will be recalled that his Duchess, who had been Mary Tribe, an old Cheltonian, was a person of many parts inasmuch as in her day she had founded and run two hospitals and was a qualified radiographer. Older readers of my book will remember her as the Flying Duchess owing to the fact that she took up flying at the age of sixty and, finally, after many exploits, alas, lost her life when she disappeared out to sea in her private plane on 22nd March 1937. The Duke, then a very elderly man, invited me to lunch at Woburn to discuss the details. It made an interesting day for me to see all its beauties, which included the deer park and his fascinating collection of birds. This was, of course, before the days of the swings and the roundabouts at Woburn.

The school year 1938–39 was a momentous one for me in various ways. First of all Lord Askwith told me that, owing to age and failing health, he had no alternative but to retire the following spring in 1939. This shook me considerably as both he and Lady Askwith had been so hospitable and friendly that I knew that this would be a gap in my life; and that they would be difficult to replace as far as both the school life and my personal feelings were concerned. I had the compensation, however, that Lady Askwith continued to be a personal friend and three of her Graham grandchildren were pupils at the College during my time as Principal.

Lord Askwith did me the honour of asking me whom I wanted as his successor. I immediately suggested someone with Canadian connections and asked whether there would be any possibility of obtaining Lord Bessborough, who had recently finished his term as Governor-General of Canada. But I did not know him personally as I had left Canada before his term started. Accordingly, Lord Askwith was kind enough to write a diplomatic letter asking him to visit the college so that we could make each other's acquaintance in the first place. He was a little afraid, as both Lord Bessborough and I were people of strong opinions who could quite easily 'blow up'; and he felt that it was an elementary precaution that we should meet in the first place.

It was an occasion of considerable joy and relief to me when, following his day's visit and a battery of questions, Lord Bessborough promised to take on the Chairmanship. He was to guide us through the awful years of the war and beyond that until his death in office during the regime of my successor, Miss Tredgold. When Lord Askwith said we could both 'blow up', perhaps he was not far from the truth. In actual fact we never did so, except on one occasion when at the end of one Council meeting he declared, 'If you do . . . I shan't remain Chairman.' I replied, 'If we don't do . . . I shan't remain Principal.' Or it may have been the other way round for all I remember of the details of our argument. Anyway, we went into the next room together and managed calmly to settle whatever it was, then started to talk of other things and came out happily together. To our surprise a number of the Council members were still about. Lord Bessborough drew me back into the room and asked, 'Why are there so many still here?' I replied, 'I've no notion. Violet Tinson is waiting for me to drive her back to Cheltenham and I'll find out.'

When all had gone except Violet and she and I went off together, I asked her the reason.

'We were afraid we might be without either a Chairman or a Principal,' she replied.

We were fortunate anyway that we did not lose our Chairman, for we could not have had a wiser, more beloved or a better one. With his background and wide connections he was able to enlist the interest of such people as Lord Ismay and Sir Charles Hambro who joined the Council. Whenever he appeared, a thrill went through the college. It is no wonder that everyone felt proud to have him. To me he was not only my Chairman but also a staunch friend, always prepared to do the best for the College and always ready to discuss a problem whether on his visits to us or if I went to see him at his home at Rowlands Castle. I can only wish that I had Lord Bessborough's gift for writing, for I have found all his books fascinating.

It was while I was spending the Christmas holidays in Jersey in 1938 with Archdeacon and Mrs. Palmer that I had a letter marked 'PRIVATE AND CONFIDENTIAL: OFFICIAL SECRETS ACT'. I opened this only to find inside another one similarly marked. As I opened this latter, I thought at least I must be guilty of some dreadful felony, involving a long term of imprisonment. However, the contents were almost as terrifying as this! For they were to give me official notification that, in event of war breaking out, all our premises at Cheltenham were to be taken over by the Government. This letter was to be merely an advance notification of this possibility. I must be ready for the event, but in the meantime I must treat this information as absolutely secret and confidential.

There was nothing for me to do in Jersey other than acknowledge the letter, while at the same time informing the writer that it was my intention to make a call at the Office of Works on my way back to Cheltenham.

On my return to London I went direct to the Office of Works, having asked the writer of my secret letter to give me a suitable appointment. You might imagine that his name would be engraved permanently on my mind, but alas, after all this time, it has escaped me. He was very pleasant but very firm; on the other hand I am always prepared to fight for what I care for and what I believe in: and I proceeded to do so. After putting up with this for a while I suppose that my interviewer thought that he must get rid of this awful woman somehow. He rang a bell and the gentleman whom I was to know later as Mr. de Norman came in to join him. I was to meet the latter some years later when we enjoyed a good laugh about the incident.

However, for the moment it was no laughing matter and I declared then: 'You won't be defending Britain if you break up the public schools.' I say it still more firmly now! After all, in 1938 the Office of Works was only trying to move us from our building, but not destroy our standards.

To return, however, to 1938, these two gentlemen of Whitehall insisted that they could not give way.

Still unconvinced, I declared, 'Well, I'll go and talk to Earl Baldwin and see if he can help.'

So, still on the warpath and taking advantage of my acquaintance with him when he had talked to us two years previously, I went along to Earl Baldwin's London house. Both he and Lady Baldwin were full of sympathy and understanding over the problem of moving 900 schoolgirls. He counselled me to wait and hope. However, he agreed with me that it was essential that I should show the letter to my Chairman, so that he could share the burden of this knowledge with me.

Here again complications ensued in the light of the impending change in this post and Lord Askwith entirely agreed that Lord Bessborough, as his successor, should be brought in owing to the fact that it was more than likely to be the latter who would have to carry the responsibility when war broke out.

It had been in the spring of 1938 that Miss Macfarlane was appointed to the Headship of St. Leonard's, St. Andrews. I was to miss her very much in the circumstances that I have just described. On the other hand, apart from her natural pleasure in such promotion, I imagine that she must also have been greatly relieved in being absolved from her task of keeping me on the straight and narrow way. A tall dignified person with a delicious academic sense of humour and an outstanding French scholar and excellent teacher and administrator, I am sure that she must have found me very tiresome. This does not mean that we did not work happily together and I learnt a lot from her. It was following the very first staff tea-party which I have mentioned that I accompanied her to her office. Arriving there I exclaimed, 'Now I suppose that I may smoke.'

Rather primly Miss Macfarlane emptied some paper clips from a small glass pot on her desk and passed it across to me. I suddenly realised that she neither smoked herself nor really approved of my doing so either.

Indeed, when term began and she found me a habitual smoker in my own room, she went so far as to suggest that would it not be better if I refrained from doing so in the presence of the girls. Unfortunately in this instance her remarks fell on stony ground. I'm not a person who can live two lives and in any case, I think that, to be honest with one's pupils and expect honesty from them, one must be one's natural self. I am sure that they would agree. I remember a group of young ones, about twelve years old, who came in one morning wanting to consult about their problems. I was sitting at my desk at the time, and one of them remarked, 'Please do smoke and sit on the stool. It is so much easier to ask all that we want to.'

On other occasions she had further reasons for disapproval. Somehow or other during the active part of my life it was always very much easier for me to run than to walk: and I often ran across the garden in the morning from my house to College. But this undignified form of activity had not in the past been *de rigeur* at Cheltenham. I remember laughing when one day I encountered an eleven-year-old coming running from the opposite direction when I was passing through Covered Way from the west wing. As we encountered each other the little girl giggled and exclaimed breathlessly, 'We shouldn't be running, but it's so much nicer, isn't it?' Unfortunately Miss Macfarlane did not show quite the same sense of amusement and indeed mentioned to me that it was perhaps to be deprecated that the Principal should be seen running at all.

Used as I was to the freedom of life in the country, I have to admit that I found it hard to adjust myself to what was to me a different way of life in the middle of a town. I well remember how my friend, Violet Andrews, niece of dear old Miss Andrews, the College historian of bygone days, would tell me the gossip with which as an invalid she was well able to keep herself informed. Violet, who combined a great sense of amusement with her capabilities as a theological scholar, told me one day during my first term how one of our local gossips had called on her and with bated breath imparted the information, 'Do you know what the Principal did last week? She was actually seen on the Promenade . . . kissing a man.' Violet explained patiently that this was an old friend, a parson from Canada who had specially come to see me. Though she was doubtful whether this had really alleviated my offence.

I was soon to learn that, in a town like Cheltenham, all the world noted everything, some perhaps with pleasure but others with disapproval!

The one thing which I really could not stand was to be told, when I wanted to wander round the College by myself, that 'The Principal is always escorted.' Mercifully, my room had two doors! One of which I was able to use to slip out unnoticed. For how in the world could one get to know the staff and the girls, still more so the domestics, unless one could go freely everywhere and alone. Fortunately, there the girls soon got used to me and were coming to my room welcoming me to their classes and houses. I soon made it clear that in my opinion there are occasions for formality and others for informality. I would not for one minute run a school if I could not have easy contact with both girls and staff.

Apart from my administrative work as Principal, I soon made it my rule to include some direct teaching by taking a number of senior Scripture classes in my own study. This too enabled me to get to know the girls as individuals and in turn the parents. I also taught two classes a week to the top two forms of Lower College, i.e. the pre-School Certificate forms. In that way I could assess their brains and capabilities and make a mental note of those from whom I might later select the senior prefects.

It was a momentous occasion for me when in July 1938 the past members of the College assembled for their Biennial Meeting of their Guild, which lasted throughout the weekend. Elizabeth Philipson-Stow, whom I have already mentioned as the General Secretary, gave me immense support on this occasion. Together we received, on the Friday evening of the assembly, the long lines of almost 600 Old Girls of the College who passed by to shake hands with us formally. She stayed beside me on the platform which was peopled with the whole of the Guild Committee, when I addressed the Guild after Prayers on Saturday, and then throughout the meetings and festivities of the weekend, I could always count on her. It was a privilege indeed to me to make so many new friends. Some, of course, of this gathering were parents of my own pupils, so that I had met them before and it was nice to see a number of faces I knew.

I well remember two amusing incidents on this occasion. First of all a very old member of the Guild came up to me to ask if I could find her 'Young Miss Ker'. I immediately sent for Margaret Kerr, aged nineteen.

'No, no,' declared my elderly interrogator, rather testily, 'it is *Sybil* Ker I want.'

I was soon to find that the adjective young was a comparative one—the Sybil Ker whom she wanted was an elderly lady, whom I only knew as a much revered member of the Council. The adjective had merely implied that the person whom she wanted was the younger of two elderly sisters.

Then on the Monday morning as the members of the Guild were dispersing, I received a distinguished general who wanted to enter his daughter to College, but who declared forcibly, 'I don't want her to become one of the stereotyped pattern.'

I told him in reply that he would just have time to move around and talk to the Old Girls before they left Cheltenham, and the present ones as well, and that I advised him to spend his day in this way and then come back and tell me what was the pattern that he wished to be avoided.

When he called back to see me in the evening, he was most amusing.

'They are all such individuals!'

What queer ideas outsiders can get of a big school!

CHAPTER EIGHT

CHELTENHAM — WAR-TIME

ᴖᴖᴖ

WHEN MISS MACFARLANE left at the end of the summer term 1938, I asked Miss Winnington-Ingram if she would stay on for a year to be Vice-Principal. The latter had been intending to retire when I first went to College but I had begged her to stay and continue as Head of Scripture. I do not think that either she had visualised herself or that anyone else had envisaged her in the position of Vice-Principal. Therefore it was a great surprise when the announcement was made; however, I am sure that my move was universally approved once everyone had recovered from this. I can well remember when I asked her to call on me during the afternoon at my house as I wanted to chat with her privately. It was then that I put my invitation to her. When she had recovered from her own surprise and had accepted the position her first remark was:

'I put on my best hat to come and see you, as I was sure you were going to ask me to retire.'

This was typical of her, for she was a great person who had served College with zest, dignity and serenity since 1912, for over thirty-five years, and was always ready to put its interests first. She was so human and possessed with such a sense of humour that she was just the person I needed to help me on the course which I had chosen to take. Above all, she was sensitive to atmosphere and we found ourselves fitting in with each other in a most admirable fashion. Maude Winnington-Ingram shared a house in Prestbury, about two miles from

Cheltenham, with a Miss Nalder who had earlier been Head of the Junior School. I often lunched with them on a Sunday and enjoyed their lovely garden, inspecting their chickens and turkeys. It was a joyous place and when we were desperate for rooms they often had girls to live with them.

Little did we know what would be before us at the end of the following year! Or that the Biennial Meeting which I described at the end of my previous chapter would be the last one for some while.

In spring 1939 I made one of my most interesting excursions abroad in company with Joan Badock. This was before she and Nora McErvel left Westonbirt to become the Heads of Gardenhurst School. This time our visit was to Tripoli in Syria to stay with Mrs. Altounian, the mother of our pupil, Yvonne Searle, who had invited me to go out there and take a friend. It was a fascinating journey travelling by the Orient Express which later, after the Golden Horn, became the so-called 'Ephesus Express' although it seemed to stop at every single station in its leisurely way across Asia Minor. All the way it made an engaging diversion to watch the storks paddling in the numerous pools and ponds that we passed, whilst the small birds flew around them. Then suddenly, with a flapping and screeching, they prepared to continue their journey northwards with the small birds nestling on their backs.

During our stay at Tripoli we were driven over to the ancient ruined city of Baalbek; it was an unforgettable experience to see the great columns against a brilliant blue sky with the morning sun shining through them. Then we travelled on to Damascus, an enchanting city to me with its 'street called straight' and its associations with St. Paul. Its clever carpet-makers and silversmiths: and the red anemones growing by the rivers Abanah and Pharphar were entrancing.

Amongst other characters we encountered on this trip was 'The Dancing Dervish' who surprisingly enough manifested himself as a dapper little man in a top hat. It seemed incredible that he was on his way out to dance in the desert.

On our return journey we stopped at Aleppo to stay with Dr. Altounian, the father-in-law of Yvonne's mother. He was a famous figure amongst all his fellow Armenians for the splendid hospital he had founded there and to which he had dedicated his life.

This was to be my last trip for some time as, by the summer of 1939, the situation was already developing in so menacing a fashion that I dare not go abroad in the summer. Accordingly, I accompanied Adeline Harmer to the Lake District, where we stayed at the Bassenthwaite Hotel. As we found ourselves rushing back from every walk to hear the news on the wireless, it seemed pointless to stay away from the College with the future so obscure. Accordingly, we returned early, I to College, she to London.

Back at Cheltenham I naturally lived from day to day in an uncertainty which amounted at times to an agonising apprehension in the light of the confidential knowledge which I possessed and which of course I had to keep to myself. It was finally on 5th September, two days after the declaration of war, that I received the official direction that the buildings of the Cheltenham Ladies' College were to be taken over by the Ministry of Works. Everything, that was, with the exception of my own house and the Bursar's office. I was adamant about one thing and that was that we should not follow the example of the Boys' College and evacuate entirely, but must still keep the nerve centre and direction of our affairs in Cheltenham. I was soon proved to be right in this as the announcement was no sooner made public than we were overwhelmed with kindness and offers of help. On my side I rang up friends in and around Cheltenham to ask if they could offer any alternative accommodation. In particular Mrs. Heber-Percy, Major and Mrs. Mitchell and Major and Mrs. Horsfall rallied round so that we were able to house the girls within reasonable distance of the College. Ninety girls under Miss Truesdale's care established themselves in Cowley Manor seven miles outside Cheltenham on the Cirencester Road, while other groups went to Brockhampton and Sevenhampton Manors all within five to six miles of the College itself. Likewise the Council agreed to taking over Seven Springs House on the Birdlip Road for the Juniors. We then acquired seven other houses in Cheltenham itself.

The rest of the young ones went to Lilleshall Manor in Shropshire which had been booked for us through the kind offices of Lord Bessborough at the time of our original scare in 1938. It had the disadvantage of being seventy miles away. However, even here there was an element of humour in the situation inasmuch as the house and grounds had been used as a pleasure ground and visiting parents found much merriment when they arrived to see the large board announcing the Pleasure Ground covered by another announcing 'Cheltenham Ladies' College' with the gold letters still to be seen below this with the words 'Fully Licensed'.

It was of course a tremendous upheaval, for we had to place the girls in each class all in the same house instead of putting those of varying ages into a house as we usually did. I owe much to the way in which the staff rallied round at this crisis. The senior members all returned prior to the start of term, established themselves in my house and worked night and day for the necessary re-organisation of time-tables and class schedules. The rest of the staff came in time to help with the moves, which was arduous work indeed.

We had to think of all kinds of expedients. For instance, I had the swimming bath, which was adjacent to the playing fields and near Christ Church, filled with water, since I took the view —which was to prove correct—that the Office of Works would at least not take that over. I kept the knowledge to myself that it could be floored over and give us a large hall opposite Christ Church where Mr. Coursey, the Vicar, allowed us to have Prayers and Scripture lessons, as well as to use the parish room for classes.

But what were we to do about classrooms? I lost no time in telephoning to the army at Bristol and asked for twenty army huts (large enough to make forty classrooms) to be sent at once.

5. Garden Party, Cheltenham Ladies' College

6. The Author and Lord Bessborough

'On whose authority?' I was immediately asked.

I was horror-struck, as this incidental aspect of the situation had not occurred to me. All I could do was to make myself appear as dense as possible and repeat over and over again, 'We've been taken over by the War Office and need twenty army huts by 3 p.m. tomorrow.' I must, however, have carried some conviction, as surely enough they appeared and were quickly put up on the playing field behind the swimming bath and filled with desks.

Thanks to the ceaseless and good-humoured work of all the house and teaching staff, College was able to open at the right time on the right date with every girl having a bed, a desk and her books settled into the right class at the right place. I have to take off my hat in particular to the parents for their co-operation in this emergency. They all received a note from me asking them to send their girls by the usual trains each with a postcard addressed back to them, so that on arrival each girl could send the name of her new house and its address back to them. They complied with this one hundred per cent and this helped to sort out the situation considerably.

I owe much to Lord Bessborough in the backing which he gave to all my actions both sanctioned and unsanctioned alike. I hope that the confidence which he placed in me during that time was not unjustified, as I think undoubtedly we were able to help the war effort considerably in giving the girls and parents a sense of stability at that critical time, when so many families were being broken up by fathers and brothers joining the Forces. Of course, my aim in acquiring houses in and around Cheltenham was to have counters with which I could bargain with the authorities. Lord Bessborough then obtained for us both an interview with Mr. Herwald Ramsbotham, M.P., First Commissioner of Works (later Lord Soulbury), who was induced to visit us. On entering my office, which was at the time in the towel cupboard of the baths, he exclaimed at once, 'You can't exist like this!' This is just what I had thought myself!

The relief was unimaginable when, after a lapse of six weeks, the main College building was returned to us in exchange for the hall in the baths—which had by then been appropriately converted according to my original plan, and the huts which I had obtained from Command Headquarters. Then I was able to proceed with the bargaining process of exchanging our temporary houses for seven of our own houses. The Lilleshall contingent was brought back at the end of term from its distant outpost and we were all once more back to normal life, except for the groups at Brockhampton and Sevenhampton who still had to come in by bus, and Miss Truesdale's group of ninety in Cowley Manor.

The numerous Cheltenham residents, such as Sir Francis Colchester-Wemys and Colonel and Mrs. de Haviland, together with many others who had lent rooms to us for our libraries and classes, once more had their houses to themselves, including those who had lent kitchens and sculleries to eke out our inadequate garden huts for the science departments. By 13th November we were fully re-established in the main College building. The black paper that the Office of Works men had put over the windows was removed and gradually the telephone wires and trestle tables that had littered the place were removed and replaced by the College tables and desks.

Meanwhile, we started to devote ourselves to an immense amount of war work in the shape of knitting, digging areas round playing fields to grow potatoes, etc. A company of the Girls' Training Corps was started, together with classes in first aid and home nursing. Many staff helped in the town with canteens and by manning air-raid shelters.

After the loss of her husband, the Head of Cheltenham Boys' College, I asked Mrs. 'Bill' Pite to follow Miss Winnington-Ingram as Vice-Principal from September 1939. Mercifully she came to us early and had understudied the latter during the summer time before being flung into the upheaval. I was most grateful for the calm with which she wrestled with all the various problems in the midst of adversity, while Miss Winnington-

Ingram, although nominally retired, was likewise always there to help in Cheltenham or at Lilleshall. Adeline Harmer came to help at Lilleshall and friends galore seemed always at hand.

Naturally, we had had our amusing moment amongst this nightmare. There were many comic episodes which were the occasion of amusement and laughter. We all learnt a great deal. What was tradition and what was merely meaningless habit became clearly distinguished from each other. Staff, girls and Guild members came to know each other more fully. Moreover, the examination results in 1940 proved clearly that these unusual circumstances had not impeded good work either at School Certificate or University Scholarship level.

I also have to pay tribute to Old Girls, for I had sent a short note round through the Guild and the response had been marvellous. Those who had not yet been called up or enlisted in war work responded with telegrams sending good wishes. Those near at hand helped in every possible way. I remember one wire from a very old member of College from Miss Beale's time—'Good! Just what Miss Beale would have done!'

We also, of course, had our own losses to the services which had to be made good. A housemistress, Mary Spence, who was an O.C., was called up to St. Thomas's Hospital; but within twenty-four hours Olive Waller, another Old Cheltonian, retired headmistress of Limuru School, Kenya, came to take her place. Alfreda Truesdale, who had come with me from Westonbirt, was outstanding. When she expressed a desire to come to Cheltenham with me I pointed out that the only vacant post I had at that moment was that of an assistant in one of the Houses. Nonetheless, nothing daunted, she came with me and was soon to take over St. Helen's House.

When the moves which I have described came about, we had to put the ninety girls working for School Certificate into Cowley Manor and it was she who took over the responsibility and remained in charge until after the war, when St. Hilda's House was returned to us and she moved back with ninety girls, thirty of whom had to be sent to Glenlee. We had all learned before the war her outstanding gift for producing plays, her ability to deal with individuals, her humour and her balance. It was a sad day when, years later, she left to take over a women's hostel at the University of Newcastle (Emily Williams Hall) and to immerse herself in the life of the university there.

Amongst other problems of September 1939 was that Miss Shaw and Miss Richards had taken a party of girls to Canada for the Public Schools Tour. When she received news of declaration of war Miss Shaw, in her wisdom, had insisted on each girl cabling her parents to ask if she should stay in Canada or return to England. How typical it was that, on receiving the cable from his daughter Jacqueline, who was to be Senior Prefect 1939–40, Sir Godfrey Russell Vick, Q.C., replied, 'Return to duty,' and kindly rang up to tell me.

Once we had some of our Houses back in November 1939 I moved out of my own Principal's House as it was large enough to accommodate one mistress and fourteen girls, and took up my new residence across the garden at the Senior House where I had two small rooms. This led to an amusing incident when Lord Bessborough rang to say that he was coming to lunch with me that day and bringing another guest with him. In my new circumstances I scarcely had either room or the necessary appurtenances for formal entertaining and, in the emergency, I enlisted the help of two clever practical prefects, Helen Trask and Katherine Grove-White. Handing them over a purse, I asked them if they could cope. I naturally had a little anxiety over this but, in the outcome, I was able on his arrival to take Lord Bessborough and his friend across to an excellent lunch, bought with discrimination and cooked and served in perfect style. C.L.C. always rises to the occasion!

There and then our Chairman, who did not fail to take in everything, announced that I should have some more accommodation. We went on a tour of investigation, in the course of which we discovered suitable rooms in the main college building for my bedroom and two visitors' rooms immediately above my study and, when our Chairman had consented to the addition of a kitchen and bathroom, I found myself fixed up with a more or less self-contained flat in the centre of the College where I lived right up to the day of my retirement. This arrangement suited me to perfection, as it made it so easy for the senior girls to come and see me in the evenings. Miss Beale in her day had also lived in College and, during the holidays, when I was alone and, of course, unable to go far in war-time, I found a great sense of peace and repose, as if her spirit was still there protecting and guiding the College which she had founded.

An alarming episode occurred during my time in the Senior House when an aerial torpedo went through a road nearby and as a consequence of the blast the whole house rose up and wavered violently. We were all assembled on the stairs at the time and someone said calmly, 'Is the house coming down?' I replied, 'Perhaps it may, so guard your heads and keep alert.' Fortunately, however, the building steadied itself without anything further happening. The only house in fact that was completely shattered at the time of this incident was one of our own, Bayshill Lawn, which was not so far returned to us, nor yet inhabited by anyone.

Running a school in war-time was anxious work, but my load was lightened considerably by the fact that, whenever there were raids about, Sir Eric Stuart-Taylor, a beloved member of our medical staff, whose daughter Lesley was Senior Prefect in 1940-41, would check round to ensure that each house was safe, even extending his activities to the three houses in the Cotswolds and would let me know. How grateful I was!

Talking about gratitude I think that, looking back on life, I am perhaps most grateful of all for having lived under Winston Churchill. Who can ever forget that wonderful speech at the time of Dunkirk when he inspired and united the whole nation? I suppose that he must have affected and carried with him every single individual in Britain by his courage, his example and his rare but unforgettable words. I well remember a member of the staff reporting to me that she had heard a prefect say to a new girl, 'No one in College is allowed to have a crush on anyone'—

then, evidently as an afterthought—'Except, of course, the Principal's for Churchill.' I often thought the girls knew me even better than I knew myself!

I certainly did my best to inspire everyone to follow him. Nor in fact did I ever try to hide my political views. Why should one be ashamed of being a Conservative, even a passionate one? But it wasn't politics then that he called for, but patriotism. It was 'England expects . . .', and this made us pour out our best efforts, however humble our job might be.

In spite of the war, thanks to the influence of our Chairman and the generosity of other great men, we still had the privilege of addresses and speeches by such distinguished people as A. D. Lindsey, Lord Bennett, former Prime Minister of Canada, Viscount Swinton, Archbishop Temple, Lieut.-General Sir Archibald Nye and Lord Bessborough himself. Also many others came to give either Lent lectures or talks on many subjects. All this outside attention together with a wide variety of different kinds of war work helped to keep education wide and balanced.

As that outstanding personality, Archbishop Temple, was lecturing entirely to young people, it seemed to me right to invite all the other schools in Cheltenham to send their boys and girls of sixteen and over to hear him when he came to see us at the beginning of autumn term 1943. I well remember how he walked on to the platform of Princess Hall holding a piece of paper certainly not more than an inch long and started his address to some 1,500 young people. Within a few moments one felt the great gathering united in spellbound attention. One could have heard a pin drop while he talked for fifty-five minutes on the dedication of the whole self to Christ and the adventure for Christ in the world. He produced the same effect on us in that hall as had Churchill on the whole country.

When I had been chatting with him before the meeting I told him that my housekeeper, who had been with me since I moved into the College building itself, had just informed me that she had had what she called 'a periodorical'. This implied that at the end of six years she felt herself compelled to leave me in the same manner as she had left the employers with whom she had been previously. Then, discovering that the Archbishop was visiting us the following term she had declared, 'You won't be able to manage him without me, so I'll stay on one more term.'

I begged him to see her and endeavour to persuade her to stay longer. Accordingly, after he had finished his talk and one of the prefects had taken him up to my quarters, the first notification of his whereabouts was when I heard roars of laughter coming from the kitchen. Sure enough, it was Archbishop Temple and my housekeeper having a get-together. He was a large man— the tale is told that, when he stepped on to a weighing machine in New York, a mechanical voice announced, 'One at a time, please.' She was nearly his size and both were possessors of that infectious laugh that penetrated in all directions. Anyway, the outcome of their chat was that I owe this very human arch-bishop not only his wonderful address, but also the fact that my Judith was to stay on with me several more years until after the war.

From this distance of time it is of more than passing interest to look back on those war-time days and what a blessing it is that the smaller comic episodes stand out in one's memory while the dreadful anxieties that beset us have fortunately been sub-merged. My companions of that time and I are filled with merriment as we call to mind the numerous incidents of all these moves which I have described in such prosaic fashion in my previous paragraphs—our staff with their cars rushing in all directions with carpet-sweepers and other household goods bulging out from windows, car boots, luggage racks and where-ever else these necessary household appurtenances could be fixed for the purpose of transit from one place to the other. We have visions of our splendid librarian, Monica Cant, one of our old girls, solemnly pushing the most urgently needed books through the streets of Cheltenham in a pram from house to house. There was the crisis in 1941 when Cowley Manor was cut off by ice and snow and had no light or phone and indeed very little water either owing to frozen pipes. Then there was the more anxious occasion when fire bombs burst on to Martin's Wood Yard and we had a naval anti-aircraft gun rushing and banging up and down Bayshill Road past the Senior Houses.

On this last occasion, as I was still living there owing to my quarters in College not being ready, I went up to see if the girls in the attic would prefer to come down to a safer and more sheltered place, but I found them all asleep. When next day I remarked to them that I had been up to see them, one of them replied: 'Oh, I did think I'd heard a noise in the night; was it you?'

I often ruminate as to why everything went so smoothly during all this time and despite all our difficulties the work had improved and examination results had been so good. I believe that it was because everyone, our Chairman and Council, parents, staff, girls and Guild were always in co-operation working for the College and the nation. There was no stinting of energy, but all worked in harmony. We regarded it as our mission to carry on all our activities just as we had done previously. All our societies continued to meet to discuss their various subjects. Concerts and lectures had continued, likewise games for those who wanted them, as well as dancing and fencing for those who preferred to take their exercise that way. Moreover, these had not detracted in any way from the energy which the girls had put into their war work, whether that of the G.T.C. or merely knitting or digging and saving.

I do not hesitate to record that one of my major problems during the war was what I can only term the American Occupation of Cheltenham. It is no aspersion on our excellent allies if I remark that my readers will appreciate my responsibilities of being in charge of the welfare of over 800 girls with the town full of American soldiers. It will be readily understood that this situation caused problems of its own in the face of which I was not able to remain inactive. The first sign of these was when it came to my notice that the G.I.s made their first impact by stopping the girls in the street and wanting to chat with them. At that moment I was thankful beyond measure that I had had a background of experience of the North American continent, and in particular for my confidence that direct action of some kind was the only solution of the problem, lest worst befall.

It was now a feature of Cheltenham life that the Americans had taken over the Queens Hotel at the top of the Promenade and only a hundred yards or so away from the College. Large numbers of them would collect inside and outside the hotel at lunchtime every day. I did the simplest and most direct thing by going into the Queens, asking to see the Officer in Charge and asking if I might talk to his men about this problem.

He was dubious of any result of this but he did arrange for them to gather into the Lounge where I addressed the multitude. In the course of what I said I explained to them that, as we were allies, I welcomed them to our midst and I did not want difficulties to arise between us. However, knowing their country and always having been struck in particular by their love of children I did want their help. I pointed out that all the girls in green uniform were my College girls and that, being responsible for them in the absence of their parents, I could not possibly allow them to talk to strangers, however charming these might be. I said that I was sure that they would appreciate my problem. From that moment onward we had no more trouble and, as the personnel changed, each batch passed the word on to the next one.

Our relationships developed on a more formalised basis when I received an approach on behalf of the Commanding Officer asking if they could borrow our hall for their entertainment one or two nights a week. I replied that our black-out of the Princess Hall was not good enough for it to be used after dark in war-time.

'But,' I added, 'shall we trade? You complete the black-out on the roof and hang good curtains over all the windows, then leave them in place when you go, and we will lend you the hall for two evenings a week.' They accepted readily and both sides gained from this bargain.

One evening General Lee, who was Commanding Officer in Cheltenham, asked me to dine with the officers quartered in the Thirlestaine Hotel. As I was familiar with the tastefully furnished rooms and the high standard of cuisine associated with the hotel in peace-time under the direction of Mrs. Lewis-Hall, the owner, I could not help seeing the funny side when I discovered that dinner was at 6.30 and that we were served with large cups of cocoa as a most unappetising accompaniment to our meat course. My longing for peace and the pleasant amenities of our English life was never stronger than when I sipped my cocoa and naturally, as the guest of honour of the occasion, had no alternative but to drink it to the last drop. However, war once over, Mrs. Lewis-Hall, after running it competently for General Lee and his officers throughout, was able to restore the Thirlestaine in peace-time once again as a first-class hotel, which proved immensely popular with parents who came down for weekends and special functions.

Another episode which amused the girls greatly was when the delightful U.S. doctors, who ran Glenlee House as a hospital during the time that the Americans were stationed at Cheltenham, invited me to lunch and called for me in a jeep. Indeed, it must have been comic to see the Principal perched up on the front seat between two members of the U.S. Army and being conveyed through the streets in this fashion.

Before ending this war-time chapter, I must give some account of the occasions that gave us the greatest joy and encouragement. These were the visits of Queen Mary who was at that time Queen Mother and who, as it will be remembered, was staying at Badminton as guest of the Duke and Duchess of Beaufort, during the war years.

Her first visit to us was a formal one on 30th May 1940, when Lord Bessborough came over to receive her and we were able to show her round the College in proper state. She took an immense interest in everything, asked endless questions while nothing went unnoticed by Her Majesty's penetrating eye. We gave her tea in my house—for I had not yet moved—and she was most delightful to us all.

A little later on, the Duchess of Beaufort rang up one morning 'out of the blue' to say that Queen Mary would like to visit us that afternoon if it would be convenient to us. The Duchess gave us the appropriate apologies and explained that it was now the rule that, while we were under threat of bombing attacks, no one had to know where Her Majesty was at any given time. Our instructions were to have all doors and gates locked except one single entrance and I must not tell either staff or girls beforehand of her impending visit. She was due at 3 p.m. and without delay I instructed all the staff and girls to attend in the Princess Hall at 2.30 before going to their afternoon classes. Naturally, these orders created a good deal of speculation, but promptly enough they were all assembled in the hall just before 2.30 while Miss Townsend, Head of the Physical Training Department, was ensuring that they all knew how to curtsy and had already started her instruction class.

At 2.35 p.m. Her Majesty arrived at the West Wing entrance and a porter rushed across to tell me.

'I am sorry, ma'am, that it all looks so empty,' I greeted her, 'but the girls are in the hall being taught to curtsy.'

'Oh,' she replied, 'what fun, do let us hurry.'

We walked rapidly across the garden and in through the open glass doors.

The entire College swept her a most beautiful curtsy and I had never seen anyone beat a retreat more quickly than Miss Townsend as she disappeared behind the stage curtain.

When the girls had gone off to their classes, Queen Mary went round everywhere and talked to everyone. While we were going round the classrooms and laboratories some of the girls curtsied while others stood to attention, while still others were not quite sure exactly what they should do.

'I'm sorry, Ma'am,' I apologised, 'that they don't all know how to greet you.'

'I enjoyed it,' she said, 'for there is so much natural courtesy and that is what matters.'

She took an immense interest in the library and gardens, where she took me to task for sounding just like Ruth Draper, the famous monologue artiste, because of my remarks that the flowers had been better a week before. What a wonderful person she was, so understanding, so natural and easy and yet always the Queen!

Her final visit to us was entirely unexpected. I had gone up the road to the bank, when one of her police-car escorts called for me. 'We've left a lady in your house,' was all they would say and offered to take me back.

On arrival, I found Queen Mary in the kitchen having a domestic chat with the cook. You can imagine the latter's delight.

Then later at tea she talked so happily and with such affection of her grandchild—our present beloved and respected Queen, who was then, of course, at school age.

Following her first visit she had presented the college library with *The Queen's Book of the Royal Red Cross* with an inscription by herself and years later she sent another gift, *My Prize-Winning Recipes*, together with pictures from Marlborough House.

She gave us so much by her visits simply because one revered her standards. Now, over thirty years later, in these horrible days when I have to shop, cook and do household chores, often before I leave the kitchen I look round and ask myself, 'Is it fit for Queen Mary to come in?' If I don't think it is up to her standard, I go back to try to make it so. Such is the impression which she left on me.

CHAPTER NINE

CHELTENHAM — POST-WAR

∾∾∾

WHEN WE dispersed for the summer holidays in 1945,
V.E. Day had been celebrated in May and throughout
the term we had shared with the whole country a
great sense of thanksgiving and relief. A large number of the
families whose head had been absent on service throughout the
war, were once more united and only those with their menfolk
out in the East were still eagerly waiting for the end of the war
with Japan. John Frith, Erica's husband, was still in a prisoner-
of-war camp; so was Eric Cordingly, who was to be our new
Rector of Leckhampton.

All the College Houses were back in our possession and, now
that life could be more free again, we were able to share the
life of the town to a greater extent. The time had come for
reappraisal and for realisation that those of us who had survived
should dedicate ourselves in gladness to widen our visions and
aim at doing the best for our country.

It was Lord Bessborough who in his talk to us in the Princess
Hall that summer of 1945, spoke briefly and clearly of 'Our
Empire Commonwealth', reminded us of this term coined by
Churchill and drew our attention to the qualities that were
required of us in order to win the peace as well as the war. He
pointed out to us that we had just as great responsibilities as we
had had during the war; and that to give of our best we needed
faith in ourselves, faith in our destiny and faith in the mission
of the Empire. How right it had been that Miss Owen had
increased her efforts in the teaching of British Empire and
American history! This talk went home to the College and

inspired courage and faith in everyone. It toned in too with the brilliant address which Canon Raven had come from Cambridge to give us the year previously on the building of the City of God. Both girls and parents had frequently remarked to me that this message had clarified their vision and strengthened their sense of purpose.

In his address on Speech Day this same year General Nye's theme seemed to point in exactly the same direction. He had emphasised the need to be proud of and to work for our British Empire. He impressed on the girls that everyone had to think clearly inasmuch as the future lay with their generation. He said that citizenship was not something merely given by the State, but that it carried duties and responsibilities as well as rights and privileges, and he impressed on everyone the need to be an Individual imbued with a joyous sense of service.

The minds of all of us were working the same way, for I had said in my own report that I agreed with Oliver Lyttelton's dictum that 'The role of the State is to create conditions in which experience, courage and the personal risk of the individual can work for the benefit of the whole'. I had urged that this country should make a place for many types of schools and that amongst them there should be the independent Public Schools with their fine tradition of learning and service. All schools should work alike for an education that would be too sincere for it to produce uniform personalities dependent on Whitehall.

Inevitably, the war over, we had a much delayed 'general post' amongst the staff and had inevitably to part with many valued members who, having loyally stayed with us throughout the war years, felt that in many instances the time had come to advance their careers by moving on to headships and other senior posts. I was sorry to lose in particular such valued members as Miss Gem who retired after having been House-lady of Fauconberg, Brockhampton Park and Roderick during her seventeen years at C.L.C., and also her second-in-command, Phyllis Wiggins.

Cheltenham—Post-War

The fact that Phyllis' father had dedicated his life to work among the lepers in East Africa meant that she had much first-hand information and a deep interest in the problems of under-developed countries. Consequently she had much to give and she and Miss Gem were great friends and worked whole-heartedly together. Both had had a splendid influence over the girls in their charge, particularly those from overseas. Of these latter we had had a number, including Chye Eng, now Mrs. Wong, from Malaya. Indeed, in 1945 we had girls from Kenya, Uganda, Egypt, India, Jersey, Gambia, Guernsey, West Africa, Tangier, Nigeria that I can think of individually, as well as others from various parts of the then British Empire, and also from France.

Mrs. Pite also had decided to leave us and become warden of a girls' club at Avon Tyrrell. As Vice-Principal she had shown herself throughout the war resourceful and ever watchful, and a tower of strength to everyone. She never seemed busy or ruffled at any time. I am so glad that now, as Mrs. Nevill, wife of the Master, she lives at Charterhouse in the City and we meet frequently.

Likewise Miss Crook's departure to become one of His Majesty's Inspectors was a great loss to the English depart-ment: her scholarship and her abiding friendliness were a personal loss to me. All these admirable people had to be replaced. Bill Pite was succeeded as Vice-Principal by Mabel Goss who had been Head of Modern Language department since 1943 and she remained with me until she left in 1950 to become Head of the Royal School at Bath.

She in turn was succeeded as Vice-Principal by Miss E. B. Clarke, who had joined the staff as Head of History in 1949. Betty Clarke is now too well known as Head of Benenden School to need any description from me. With her brilliant brain, legal and historical knowledge and delicious sense of humour she guided and helped me in every way through these last years before my retirement in 1953. I can never be sufficiently grateful to her and I enjoy meeting her whenever our paths cross.

It was much compensation when in September 1947 Miss A. K. Clarke rejoined me. She had been in College since 1924 and had been Head of Classics and of the University Entrance, until she left for a year in order to become temporary Director of Classical Studies at Newnham College, Cambridge, a post which gave her more facilities for research for her forthcoming book than if she had remained at Cheltenham. Even during that year we missed not only her scholarly teaching, but her personality, wisdom and sound judgment. It was a joy to us when she came back for six more years which she subsequently told me were the happiest years of all, inasmuch as she had no serious responsibilities and was able to devote her time to teaching the senior girls and continuing her research. Now once again she is coaching in Cambridge, and it was only the other day she told me of two more books that she hopes to have ready for publication shortly.

It would be wrong of me if in this context I did not mention also those who had played such an important part during the war, who included such friends as Elizabeth Wills-Browne and Alfreda Truesdale. Likewise, there was Margaret le Maître who came as Head of Modern Languages in 1941. Maud Kidney, who had been secretary at Westonbirt, where our lifelong friendship began, took over the Secretarial Department in 1941, while Mlle Favre—who had been with me both at Havergal and Westonbirt—joined the Modern Language staff in 1942; then in 1945 Joyce Biddle, who after Westonbirt had been Head of Classics for five years at Oxford High School, took over the Headship of the Classics Department from A. K. Clarke.

Another great character who left us during this time owing to age and ill health was Miss Scrivener who, formerly an actress, had taught voice production. It was my early dealings with her that cemented the relationship between us during her time at College. Before the start of my first term I asked her to come with me to the Princess Hall and tell me to which part I should direct my voice from the platform in order that I should be heard throughout the hall. She replied dogmatically: 'There is

7. Peter

8. The Author and Sir Charles Hambro receiving guests

no such place.' I insisted that I must have her advice. 'Well, if
the Principal says I must, I suppose I must.' she replied. Feeling
very squashed, I still insisted. Accordingly, she came, tested me
and was delighted when she found that I could be heard clearly.
We had tea together and were friends from then on. She was an
unusual-looking woman and no one except her doctor knew if
her hat was on her curls or her curls attached to her hat, for she
invariably wore a largeish hat and brown coat with a cape!
Nonetheless we all admired her and she was a loss to us when
she departed.

An important person to return after the war was Weaver—
the College engineer whom we had appointed shortly before
war broke out and who had left us to rejoin the R.N.V.R. He
was devoted to dogs and looked after my Peter in the holidays
and daily took him for early exercise during term-time. He and
Mrs. Weaver are still in College and it is splendid to see them
again each year when I visit.

In the natural course of things we had changes in the Council
of the College and its administration. I was delighted when Sir
Kenneth Clark joined the Council and College gained so much
from his delightful art lectures which he gave so generously over
the years. I suffered the loss of my friend 'Chips' Fraser who had
to give up the Council. She was fortunately replaced by the
charming and capable Diana Ryder, wife of Hugh Ryder, as
my representative, and I was able to count on her so much
throughout the years, so that her death in 1951 was a great
shock and sorrow to me. Her daughter, Jane, and her nieces,
Caroline and Penelope Makins, were in the College during my
time.

It was in 1945 that Colonel Tarrant, whom I have already
mentioned as our Bursar, retired at an advanced age and was
succeeded by David Leighton who, on returning from the Forces,
was well equipped for the necessary modernisation of our
Bursar's office and its adaptation for dealing with the pressures
of the modern age. Dear Colonel Tarrant, old-timer that he was,
had never thought filing cabinets essential and was in the habit

of keeping all his documents, including the entrance forms for the girls, folded up in Gladstone bags.

We were also fortunate in the appointment to the Council of Dr. Costley-White, former Head of Westminster School and then Dean of Gloucester. An event of equal importance to C.L.C. was that of the retirement of Bishop Headlam, when the See of Gloucester was taken by Bishop Woodward, my friend of Westonbirt days. Only a few days after his enthronement he took Prayers at College and gave a short inspiring address. His gift with young people is too well known to need any emphasis by me, but I must mention how delighted I was to have him on the Council. The fact that he came to us so soon and again a little while later meant that he got to know both staff and girls; and from that time we looked forward to most inspiring Confirmation addresses from him.

I was, however, sorry to see Bishop Headlam depart. I think of him with affection and gratitude even though I could never persuade him to give shorter and more inspiring Confirmation addresses. In fact there is one very funny episode that stands out in my mind in connection with this. This was the year when we had had some candidates ill with infectious diseases at the time of Confirmation and he, with his usual kindness, after the Easter holidays took a special service at Leckhampton Church. We had by this time grown accustomed to his warning, 'I do not want to see any lapsed Confirmation candidates,' prefacing his last sentence. So that at this particular service both choir and congregation began to stand as soon as they heard these words, only to find that he had several more sentences to follow.

An immediate feature of the post-war period was the number of applications for entry which I received from all parts of the world from parents who had encountered old Cheltenham girls in far-off places and admired the qualities that they had evidenced as a result of their school education. At the same time 1945 and 1946 brought a great influx of families returning home from overseas. Their girls brought new experiences and their fresh ideas were a great asset to the school. I, too, benefited

146

in my personal life inasmuch as many of the parents became firm friends.

In particular I can think of John and Margot Taylor who are associated with my first post-war journey abroad, inasmuch as in 1945 John (now Sir John) Taylor was in the Diplomatic Service and posted to the embassy at Cairo.

It was natural that after the restrictions of war we should all begin to talk of travel and it was in 1946 that Pat Ellis' mother invited me to Tangier for August. Pat and her friend, Felicity Jameson, were both going on to the university and as the latter also was going to Tangier, we all decided to fly out together.

What a great joy the sun and colour of Tangier, its beauty and freedom from restrictions was to me after the long years of 'blackout' in England! I enjoyed that colourful land perhaps more than I had done at any time in my life. The Ellis family took us all over the region, amongst both Moors and Arabs and to distant places where we could rejoice in the wide spaces of the desert and the distant view of the mountains.

Hearing that I would be in Tangier Sir Arthur and Lady Richards (now Lord and Lady Milverton) invited me to Lagos where he was Governor. I have often regretted that shortage of time did not allow me to accept this invitation, for to have seen Nigeria then would perhaps have given one more understanding of the situation today. We had made friends when they had brought their golden-haired Diana to College after the war. Educated in various places from Fiji to Havergal, Diana was very much an individual, a person to be led by reason and not dragooned. After settling in, she made her mark at College, was Head Girl of Hatherley Court, became a good historian and went on to Westfield.

However, I did not get to Nigeria; but, before leaving Morocco from the Casablanca airport, I did manage to visit the beautiful white-housed French town of Rabat, ablaze with its rambler roses. Then I flew on to Cairo to see the Taylors and spend the summer with them. But how small the world sometimes is! Our plane unexpectedly had to descend at Algiers and

I found myself deposited in the most dreary and horrible Customs House imaginable. When the Customs Officer wanted to open my cases I said, 'I'm like melting butter, please do the other people first.' Then, when the others had passed through, I gave him a cigarette and begged him to bond my cases straight through to the Cairo embassy. In the meantime a few people had come in and I exclaimed in desperation, 'Is there any Cheltonian here?' A pleasant voice replied: 'I fear not. Would Eton do?' That kind Etonian took me to the only hotel open in the heat of the summer, got me enough Algerian money to pay for my room there and then drove me on to the English Library with the information that the two sisters, whose brother was Librarian, had been at C.L.C. in Miss Beale's time.

These two ladies gave a splendid welcome to this unexpected stranger and were kind enough to act as my hosts during the short time that I was in Algiers. I think it is one of the happiest things in life to meet people in out-of-the-way places with whom one has associations in common. Oddly enough, when I got back to the airport, I ran into the son of Mr. Truman of Truman and Knightly's Educational Agency.

After the heat, dust and dirt of Algiers how good it was to be met by John Taylor at the Cairo airport! We were passed through Customs and Immigration without formalities and driven to join Margot and the two girls, Millicent and Grizel, in their charming house on the outskirts of the city. Both girls were then in College but are now married.

It was a joy to see the life of Cairo in those days. I had been there for a very short time before the war with Sybil Neville-Rolfe after staying with Miss Gribble near Ismailia. This time, however, I met the embassy world and went with Margot to visit the lovely markets where I could feast my eyes on all the glorious silks and brocades and buy a few presents to bring home to friends. After seeing the various sides of Cairo life I went by car across the desert, the road still being marked out by petrol cans, to Alexandria. Again I found great hospitality with the Philps whose elder girl had been in C.L.C. all through the war and the younger one due to enter. I stayed with Miss Bloxham, Head of the English School for Girls and amongst other entertainments enjoyed the cocktail party given by Judge and Lady Holmes, C.L.C. parents. It was truly a refreshing summer.

However, peace-time brought its problems as well as its pleasures. From my first year at College I had been convinced that we ought not to have a Junior Department attached to the College as it was my opinion that no girl should be in the same school from kindergarten to university level. However, with the war pending, it was impossible to make specific arrangements then. By 1944, however, it had become the Ministry of Education's policy to have a division at eleven plus and the Hadow Report had advocated this.

Accordingly, as soon as the war was over, it was the moment to act and the Council, on my advice, bought Bredenbury Court in Herefordshire, thirty miles away, as a Preparatory Boarding School. This created no end of a furore amongst the parents of the day Juniors who had had the advantage of attending College and were incensed at the thought of me depriving them of this opportunity. However, I did everything possible to recommend the several other junior schools in the town and I think that eventually they realised they were taking too narrow a view.

In any case we simply had to have the space for the senior girls in the west wing classrooms and Hatherley Court for senior boarders. But in the meantime the situation had not been without its strains, though I could not help seeing the funny side of it as I stood alone on the platform at the meeting called to explain the change, whilst parents of the deprived Juniors attacked me, looking for all the world as if they were gathered together ready to throw stones at me.

In October 1946 Lord Bessborough gave us a talk on behalf of the Franco-British Society and this was prefaced by an account from Felicity Jameson of the experiences and impressions of a group of boys and girls who had toured the battlefields of France under his guidance. He told us how Mr. Churchill, though heavily occupied night and day in directing the war effort of Britain and her allies, had emphasised in the House and elsewhere that a strong and friendly France was a major British interest. Needless to say, College responded and Miss Le Maître built up a vigorous branch of the Society in Cheltenham.

I must not leave 1946 without mentioning the pleasure given by our having procured our own cinema. It was inaugurated by a showing of *The Young Mr. Pitt* followed on a wet Saturday half-term holiday by *Forever England*, and much appreciated by parents and girls alike. It has been of great use ever since.

By 1947 life had become normal again and we organised our routine that in alternate years we would have the Guild Biennial at the College in summer term one year and Speech Day the alternate one. In this year we were fortunate enough to have Princess Alice of Athlone who talked on 'Courtesy'. Now that life was more peaceful we had many talks from eminent men. Quite the most popular of these was Kenneth Clark, whose brilliant daughter during those years progressed steadily up the College, finally being my Senior Prefect in 1950–51. She had many gifts and much personality, being always the same whether in College or in her extremely artistic and beautiful home. Also when her Entrance Exams to Oxford were over and she was Senior Prefect, she could go up to London for her presentation at Court and coming-out dance, but was always back promptly from these occasions, once again in uniform and fulfilling her duties in single-minded fashion. She certainly could walk with kings and not lose the common touch and now she has made her name in the artistic and literary world.

Another literary parent who gave us immense pleasure by his talks and poetry readings was Richard Church and it was always a joy to see him and Mrs. Church. I hope one day that I shall see Janet Church again, but she married and went to Canada soon after leaving school and now I think that she and her husband are at Victoria University in New Zealand.

Then too there was that cheerful literary vagabond S. P. B.

Mais, who was a not infrequent lecturer when Lalage and Imogen were in College. Lady Forbes also gave us delightful talks on South Africa where she was born and bred, and on Portugal which she knew so well. We all agreed that she had the capacity to describe places in such a way as to enable one to visualise and long to visit them.

These post-war years also gave the girls the opportunity to get to know the beautiful Cotswold country that was on our doorstep and groups of the older girls would go on expeditions to do brass rubbings, go flower hunting and visiting beauty spots. In 1948 we had one very great sadness—Pamela Jowsey was killed one Sunday morning while bicycling to church at Gloucester Cathedral. I went through great heart-searching wondering whether her parents would think that I should not have let them bicycle along the busy Cheltenham to Gloucester road. Should I forbid the girls to go out in small groups? On the other hand would it be right to curtail their freedom? Words could not express my gratitude to her parents for their kindly forbearance. There was no word of blame at all. In fact they reassured me that it was the only thing to allow the girls to take some risks if they were to accustom themselves to the conditions of freedom in which they would have to live their lives in the future. In their grief they worried most about the effect the tragic incident would have on Pamela's twin, Jenifer; for, although the twins were very different from each other, they were the closest of friends. However, Jenifer went on to Oxford and having inherited, I suppose, good scientific ability from her brilliant father, she gained a Ph.D. and has excelled in life. A humble-minded scholar, she has always been a great worker and her mother tells me that she was nominated amongst others for a Nobel Prize. Now, after publishing works on scientific research and radioactive isotopes, she has become the greatest authority on Osteoporosis and has been called from America, where she is Assistant Professor at Minneapolis University to visit South Africa and France to see special cases.

Boring—Never!

During the post-war years it was easier to encourage initiative and the development of individual interest than it had been during the years of the war. College always was one great family comprising girls of outstanding ability whose interests were academic and those whose capacity lay largely in other directions and whose personalities developed best with wide but less academic forms of teaching, as, for instance, Eve Lovell, who became a world champion at ice skating, a good singer, an excellent needlewoman and artistic in many lines and who is now married and bringing up her children.

It was for such girls that, in 1946, I had started the Citizenship Class, so that after they had taken the G.C.E. 'O' level, those most suited for such a course would concentrate on local and national history, learn about the various forms of social work, and have good practical lessons in domestic science. They also visited various kinds of institutions and studied local government. In this way, these girls learnt to work with as much enthusiasm as their more academic friends. They joined a cadet company of the Guides where they had training in leadership, learnt First Aid and Home Nursing and had to pass the appropriate examinations with a view to rendering service wherever it was needed. I believe that every young person reacts best to training and education if his or her interest is awakened to world needs, while at the same time he or she has as much freedom as possible to develop his or her own tastes and capabilities.

Being completely unmusical myself I was intensely grateful for the direction of Dr. Sumsion, Miss Runge and others of the music staff. Miss Rowley's production of *H.M.S. Pinafore* was the first of many brilliant performances and our actors and musicians played a most important role in the life of the College which culminated during my own time in the Chronicle Play at the Centenary in 1953.

By 1950 I was more than due for a Grace Term which (for the information of those unfamiliar with our ways) means that I was privileged to take a term off on full pay for the purpose of travel and pursuing my own bent. However, the Council decided that, instead of this, they would give me seven weeks, two of these before the Easter holiday and one after, and would pay my fare to fly the round trip out to America and back home from Canada. This, as far as I was concerned, was an acceptable alternative. Sir Charles Hambro made all my arrangements which included my being met and entertained first of all in New York where I was shown round the city with its many new skyscrapers and also had the opportunity of visiting the old Cheltenham girls who were living there.

I went next to stay with the Taylors in Washington, where John had been moved during the intervening time since I had seen them in Cairo. Washington provided a real surprise for me as I had not been there since 1928 and many changes had taken place in the meantime—not all for the best. All the same the Potomac and the State buildings still retained their beauty. Margot was kind enough to take me round in the same manner as she had done in Cairo—our round included a private school in Virginia, and a visit to the home of Sir Oliver Franks who was then our Ambassador.

From Washington I went to stay with friends in Ottawa before going to Toronto to see the Dale-Harris family and others: and I much enjoyed staying with Douglas and Aileen Wood in Rosedale. It was a happy time for me but nonetheless Canada also had changed much and I am glad that I first knew it in its less industrialised days in the 1920s. After a night with Agatha and Penn Patterson in Montreal I flew home refreshed and ready for further strenuous times ahead.

We had for long enough been awaiting a full inspection of the school by the Ministry and I had been asking for this over a matter of years. However, now they finally decided to visit us. It was an inopportune time inasmuch as we already had our arrangements for the 1953 Centenary of the College in hand. However, we could not have wished for a better report. The inspectors told me in particular how frank they found the girls. One twelve-year-old had escorted one of them to a House for lunch and *en route* enquired why they inspected schools. Then she went on to volunteer the information, 'If you want what Pops—I mean Miss Popham—doesn't think right, she won't do it.'

In 1952 I told Lord Bessborough that, as soon as the Centenary celebrations were over, I must retire. He tried to persuade me not to, until I said bluntly, 'I did not want to take the appointment of a large school in the first place, but I did so because I thought that it was right. I've loved every minute of it and I shall hate to leave. But again I do so because I think it right.' He understood my attitude and supported me when I made my formal statement to the Council. I had decided to leave after nearly seventeen years because I knew that I had given of my best and I could not think of staying on if I no longer had the energy and enthusiasm to be able to learn to know every individual pupil well.

The whole of my last year was filled with the excitement of looking forward to the Centenary weekend when we had decided to combine Speech Day and the Guild Biennial Gathering. What preparations there were! Especially for the splendid play written and produced by Peggy Challis, who was then House Lady of Fauconberg House and is now Head of Queen Anne's School, Caversham. How she managed a cast of 200 girls and many boys from the Boys' College, I do not know! It portrayed the history of the emancipation of women during the century 1853–1953 in what in the title was termed 'a light-hearted interpretation'. The performance, which took place three times over the weekend, was a great success right from its opening with Miss Maude Winnington-Ingram in the role of Miss Beale dressed just as she was represented in the Shannon portrait, with which we were so familiar.

However, a full account of the Centenary Weekend is on record in the Centenary Number of the *Magazine* and I cannot do better than reproduce the short account by Lady Tweedsmuir that appeared in this number under the title 'Parents and College'.

'One of the great qualities of College is that, as a parent, one can look forward to a visit sure of a warm welcome, not only from one's daughter, but from the Staff, Principal and, one really feels, all the unknown girls as well. I am sure that was the common experience of the many hundreds of parents visiting College for the Centenary Weekend.

'I was greeted on arrival by the Council and Miss Popham, looking far too slight and young to retire, in an elegant grey dress and a becoming hat trimmed with roses. I had a huge luncheon in a gay red and white marquee with the sixty-five other guests and members of the Council. Fortified by this, I stood in the marble corridor, watching the lines of girls in green moving swiftly and silently towards the Princess Hall. Then it was our turn to take our places in the vast Hall, whose stage was magnificently decorated with huge delphiniums. The body of the Hall and lower galleries were filled with parents, Old Girls and friends in their cheerful summer frocks, shown at their best against the dark walls. High in the top galleries the silent stillness of the girls was in striking contrast to parents' chatter.

'At last "they" came. Lord Bessborough, Chairman of the Council, Miss Florence Horsbrugh, Minister of Education, the Council and "Pops". The great occasion began. The Minister spoke of the School Inspectors' Report.

"The College is unique among girls' boarding schools in England in its size and in the volume of its advanced work. . . . it would be difficult to overrate the sound scholarship and the spirit of strenuous disciplined effort, both in work and behaviour, which have long been traditions of the College and which are being so well maintained by the present generation of staff and girls."

'Lord Bessborough, deeply moved by the Principal's retirement, reviewed the 100 years. Then came Miss Popham, with characteristic courage meeting emotion with a laugh, turning as always to the future—I think we all admired her then— and afterwards the call for three cheers from the Senior

Prefect, and if at that moment some in that great audience fought back the poignant past, it was due to the expression in that girl's voice, of loyalty to the Principal. It is not easy to combine the rejoicing of a centenary and a farewell.

'For the moment, the Centenary Weekend was a joyful gathering in brilliant weather. There were 3,300 at the Garden Party, which might have been one of the Coronation Receptions to overseas visitors, with girls from Africa, Malaya, America, Europe and the Dominions. What a tribute to the College that it is "the best-known independent girls' school in the world"! The test of any effective Institution in this country is whether it attracts people from beyond the shores of Britain. The fact that girls from the Orient come to Cheltenham for their studies is an interesting mirror of changes in the status of women taking place in their own countries.

'The history of College under the guidance of four famous Principals has been marked by steady achievement in academic distinction. This is a proud record in a century which has seen the struggle for general literacy supplant the tradition of a highly educated few. And how many will judge themselves literate by the standard of those days, described by Lord Chesterfield in the eighteenth century, when he claimed that a really literate man was one who could read and write Latin and Greek fluently! Yet today exams get harder. There is no doubt that over the years the standard expected and reached at College is becoming steadily higher.

'No one doubts the College reputation to instil learning. The results of studies were seen at the Centenary Weekend in many exhibits of work. What of the more human qualities? Competitions of all kinds were evidence of training in sport. But it was at the various Houses that one sensed the family atmosphere. Here was the counterbalance of family life to the discipline of work. Indeed, at one College House several parents' caravans were parked!

'This sense of home in the midst of a College noted for serious study is a great achievement, the true balance between the gay and serious. It also reflects the mid-twentieth-century attitude to things feminine. In early days women were feminine and dependent—the time when for a woman to read an advanced classic was to call forth the remark, "Don't let a man see you reading that." Then, as women fought and won their rights in a civilised country, they were inclined to become somewhat severe and masculine. How they have settled down to a happy mixture—a perfect example is found in Miss Popham. Then there is Miss Rose Heilbron, Q.C., a brilliant barrister, but most attractive, too. The modern woman does not spurn domestic pursuits. She learns to manage her home, remain feminine, but, because she has wider interests and often an outside job as well, she is an intelligent companion to her family and friends. In essence it is the desire for partnership between men and women in all the adventures of life.

'Because the next twenty years will probably be the most important at this testing time, it means that those girls still at College now will be able to do something about it. Parents may have some faith that their own children can hold the future safely in their keeping. For at the Centenary Weekend the various official functions ended with a religious service conducted by the Bishop of Gloucester. A generation cannot go far wrong which builds upon a strong religious foundation. So it is that, thinking over all that College has to offer, and asks of those who study there, I, as a parent, am content.'

I will only say that it was a unique occasion to the 3,300 Old Girls, friends, parents and contemporary members of the College—and, lastly, to myself. A few days later an elderly road workman passed the comment to me, 'Say, ma'am, all this part o' Gloucestershire was stuffed full of your College folk, and what a fine lot they were.'

One moment that moved me greatly was when Miss Florence Horsbrugh, Minister of Education, who was our guest of honour, in her speech on the Friday talked of the Inspectors' Report and

remarked, 'It would be difficult to overrate the sound scholarship and the spirit of strenuous disciplined effort both in work
and behaviour which are being so well maintained by the
present generation of staff and girls.' I felt that I had not striven
in vain.

An even more terrible moment was the ceremony on Saturday
morning when Lord Bessborough unveiled my own portrait by
A. R. Thompson. It was then that I realised what it would
mean to me to leave the College that I loved so much and how
much I should miss working with our beloved Chairman.

Also I had to make my farewell speech as President of the
Guild and when I came to take my last leaving Prayers I knew
that this was going to be a more anxious occasion even than my
first one.

However, the main thing was the future of the College and to
make this Centenary Weekend one to be remembered in its
Thanksgiving for our life and all its joys. On the Sunday the
Bishop of Gloucester—our much-loved 'Woody'—took a Service
in the Princess Hall; this, as may well be imagined, was packed
to capacity while it was also relayed to all the other halls which
were equally full.

After my 'good-bye' to parents and Old Girls our weekend
closed. However, as there was just a short time left before the
end of term and I was determined that my final farewell to the
girls should be happy, I decided to give a dance for the prefects
and all Upper College leavers. Thus they had the excitement of
writing to brothers and friends at the Boys' College, at Marlborough and other Public Schools, and collecting their dresses
and everything else that was needed for a dance. In this way
the end of the academic year of 1953 was a joyful occasion in
addition to a farewell.

Under such memorable circumstances I left Cheltenham
where, for fifty terms, College and the care of individuals
associated with it had been my life. It had been a wonderful
fellowship—Council, teaching staff, Houseladies and girls—
and parents too.

Cheltenham—Post-War

It has invariably made me happy when I have been able from time to time to welcome any of them at my London flat when, as so frequently happens, they have paid a call on me. I hope that they will continue to do so.

CHAPTER TEN

RETIREMENT

∽∽∽

As my retirement approached I had naturally toyed with the idea, which is so common to all professional people, of living in a cottage in a country village. However, as the time approached I realised more and more that I would have difficulty in adjusting to village life and I had some difficulty in imagining myself a regular weekly attender at the Women's Institute! I felt that I would rather be a small, though independent, pebble in a big pool! Accordingly, a year before my retirement, with the help of kind Mr. Franzini, whose Barbara was in college, I took a nice little flat in Queens Gate Place. Maud Kidney and I had decided to live together and this gave us a *pied-à-terre* from which to hunt for a future residence where we could finally settle. However, in spite of all our sales of furniture and thousands of books, when we arrived we were so smothered by our remaining possessions that we felt that we could go no further. London seemed the obvious place to live where friends could call on us and be entertained and, if we ever should come to be bored, there were theatres, galleries and endless other interests.

Fortunately perhaps for Maud, I was no sooner free of my Cheltenham responsibilities than I was invited on a fortnight's lecture tour to Denmark to talk about the English Public Schools. Looking back, I am sure that I ought to have asked for this to be postponed for a year, for following the Centenary and my move I was too tired to take on the responsibility of undertaking talks as well, and could have done them very much better at a later date. However, I suppose that action is irresistible to me and accordingly I flew to Copenhagen to be met by the head of the Danish-British Society and our Consul, Mr. Bishop, and I was sent straight to Aalborg in the north of Jutland, where I was delightfully entertained by some very likeable English people who gave me basic information about Denmark. I had not appreciated that a so substantial and important part of the country was situated on islands and that, in order to get from Copenhagen to Aalborg, it involved so much crossing from one island to the next.

I then travelled south through Aarhus, the university town, and Vejle but, while I was lucky in my hostesses, I never got sufficient information from them to enable me to make any useful comparison between British and Danish education. At Aarhus my host took me round the famous Old Town, rather like a small island inside the town, which was comprised entirely of furnished wooden houses of the fifteenth century. I understand that this had been formed by houses moved from all parts of the country and arranged as a complete replica of a mediaeval village. I then visited Odense on the island of Fünen, the birthplace of Hans Christian Andersen. From there, travelling through Hillerod and other towns, I returned to Copenhagen after seeing a number of schools and educational establishments.

I did not have the time to prove their fundamental ideas, but I had the impression that religion did not play a very large part in the Danish educational system and likewise that there were not only fewer boarding schools, but those which I saw were not at all like our Public Schools. Also they had more co-education than we did and what I saw of this in Denmark left me with the same impression as I had gained in Canada and U.S.A. I still think that it is good for the sexes to mix up to the age of eleven or so and after seventeen, but girls and boys develop so differently during their teens that, especially if they can mix together during the holidays, I do consider that our segregated public school system is the best.

After the final stage of my journey through rain and across

water—it seemed a case of water, water everywhere—I was met again at Copenhagen, cold and weary, by Mr. Bishop and the head of the Danish-British Society and taken by the former to his house. Here we had a small reception, amongst the guests being a pleasantly mannered Wykehamist. It was 10 p.m. and Mrs. Bishop provided us with whisky and sandwiches—all most welcome. I had naturally regarded this occasion as a private one and conversation flowed accordingly without my realising that, in the young gentleman I have mentioned, we had a newspaper reporter in our midst. I was all the more surprised when on the day I left Denmark, one of our morning papers came out with a large headline 'LATE HEADMISTRESS OF CHELTEN-HAM WITH BLUE HAIR DRANK WHISKY AND DECLARED ALL GIRLS ARE SEX MAD'. I imagined the horror of some of the more staid and elderly in Cheltenham! I lost no time in phoning Lord Bessborough on my return but he advised, 'Ignore it. Probably a sub-editor trying a stunt.' And so it was! There was nothing wrong in the original report —it was the slanting of the headlines which was objectionable.

I enjoyed my final days in Copenhagen during which time I was taken out on an excursion to see the castle at Elsinore—a wild place on a stormy day in which one could well envisage the gloomy Dane still walking the battlements. I loved the statue of the mermaid at Copenhagen and never think of Denmark without visualising her at the entrance to the harbour. I was also fascinated by the Copenhagen china factory and all its beautiful figurines of animals and children, one of which has been given me by an Old Cheltonian who was aware of my love for beautiful china. After enjoying the entertainment given by our Ambassador and by notable Danish people, I gave my last lecture and flew on to Paris where my friend, Comtesse de la Calle had begged me to spend the first fortnight of term with her at her finishing school. As there happened to be a group of Old Cheltonians there at the time, this was a lot of fun for me. However, my friend was herself ageing and finding the girls difficult and now her niece has taken over the school, modernised it and made it an excellent place for girls who want to spend a term in Paris and learn more French before university and a career.

Then on Boxing Day of 1953 I left for my first visit to India of which I shall have to tell in the appropriate place in my next chapter. It was only on my return that Maud and I found the occasion to start hunting for a larger place, which we finally found in a top flat in Albert Hall Mansions, into which we moved in November 1954. It was a gracious and pleasant place in which we each had our own bedroom and sitting-room and we were to stay there until October 1965.

I can truthfully say that in my retirement—though perhaps that is hardly the correct word for it!—I have found much to interest me along the lines of my deep-rooted interests in politics, travel and education. Throughout my accounts I have endeavoured to make some mention of my travels and now my new freedom gave me a fresh urge both to visit new places and to familiarise myself to a greater extent with the old ones, in the manner which I hope to describe in my Chapter Twelve.

However, I did not lose interest in my devotion to educational work and I have been throughout the years interested in the Executive of the Governing Bodies of Girls' Schools and so keep in touch with the changing problem of a new age. In particular I fight as hard as I can to resist State interference in the Public Schools, for it is the diversity and independence of these schools which imbues young people with individuality and proper standards, so that, as they grow up, they are able to give wise leadership in the present time of turbulence and rapid change. Whilst I believe in modernisation and the development of technology, I have made it clear that I believe in tradition also. In these days it is my view there is too great a tendency to throw out the baby with the bath-water—especially as far as the world of education is concerned.

In addition to this general interest I have also been fortunate in being able to take special interest in three different schools. Until last summer I was a Governor of Cleveland School in

163

County Durham where Rene Chalmers, an Old Cheltonian, though before my time, claimed me at once as soon as she saw I was free. I agreed readily because I admired the way that, from having a few children in her house, she had built up a really sound school of over 300 girls and developed it into a Public Day School. She gave the right religious basis to education, was in constant touch with parents and aimed at high intellectual standards in order to prepare her girls for careers.

Esther Torkington did much the same, but has chiefly boarders. Our respective fathers knew each other in the Diocese of Southwark many years ago, while her elder sister and I were at Westfield together, and I often saw her younger one when I was at Westonbirt. So when, after her husband's death, Esther asked me to be a Governor of Croft House School, Shillingstone, I agreed. The atmosphere of this school which lies amongst wide grounds in the beautiful countryside of Dorset is permeated by her goodness.

The third school of which I am Governor and Chairman is an outstanding Preparatory School, Kenton Court, Rottingdean, near Brighton. The Head is Kathleen Birney who is now helped by one of her sisters who was a housemistress at the Godolphin School, and another who has recently retired from being Head of the Clergy Daughters' School at Bushey. Though a small school, it produces remarkable results. Whenever a parent has asked me, 'Where can I send my child to ensure that she will go on to such and such a Public School?' I always recommend Kenton Court and without exception it has justified my recommendation. Parsons' daughters, all these sisters are born educationalists. It is the happiest school imaginable, because there is a proper balance of freedom and discipline both of which I believe to be essential. They give such sound and inspiring teaching that the young things love to learn and have the right sense of curiosity to do so.

Education, however, is not confined to schools and I think that quite my most interesting activity has been connected with Westfield College on whose Council I have been the whole time

from 1935 until last Christmas. On coming to London I soon
found myself active on many of its committees, the most exciting
being those that dealt with new buildings. I had loved Westfield
in its days as a small college exclusively for women. However,
times change and I am convinced that it was right to build the
new science blocks to increase the number of residencies and to
bring in men. Much has been done in this respect and there are
future developments in hand in the planning of which I am
happy to have taken some part. All my contacts with the College
rejoice me and I am glad to have served on the Council long
enough to have had contact with the clever and delightful new
Principal, Dr. Bryan Thwaites, Ph.D. I have enjoyed working
under all the chairmen and perhaps especially under Gerald
Ellison, Bishop of Chester, who also retired at the same time as
I did in 1966. Though I am no longer active, I still visit the
College and go to functions there.

To turn from education to politics I was pleased to be invited
to serve on the Conservative Women's National Advisory Committee, for I have always been a keen Conservative. Why?
Because I believe it has been the Party that cares most for
Britain, that is really patriotic and has the majority of people
with judgment. I believe they stand in the country for what I
have stood for in schools, i.e. the preservation of true traditions
combined with a forward-looking attitude and a readiness to
make changes when desirable. They have not the passion to
level *down* as do those who are motivated by envy, hatred and
malice, nor are they class conscious. I enjoyed working on the
Queen's Gate Executive and the South Kensington one. At
present I am not professing to work, but at the G.L.C. Election
I did manage to stir up twenty to thirty people to vote, who
had said that they did not think local elections mattered. I do
not cease to carry on my propaganda in the shops and all round
this district. One old man whom I meet regularly always greets
me, 'Morning, Blue Lady.'

I am a Tory also because I think that they care more for the
Commonwealth, as does the Executive of Commonwealth

Migration Council, on which I served from 1956–66 when I resigned, as I think younger people are needed. When they sent out young people to work overseas for the summer vacation, I persuaded Marina Orr to go to Canada and also Susan South, an Old Cheltonian who was then at Westfield where she gained a First in Spanish. Another Old Cheltonian who went out to Canada was Janet Roseveare, but in her case she went independently. She worked first with the Bell Telephone Company and later turned to teaching. She had been an excellent senior prefect at college and came from an educational family. Since her return she has added a mathematics degree to her Cambridge B.A. in Classics and is still teaching. Another Old Cheltonian adventurer is Margaret Evers, who went out to Australia and then on to Papua where she started a school in a goatshed, but now has a good building, competent staff and some 300 children. In these days, however, one does not have to urge migration! Too many are anxious to escape all the present Government's restrictions.

Having spent my life in independent schools, encouraging pupils to learn history and to take interest in current affairs, local government and politics, it was natural that in 1954 I should join the Society for Individual Freedom. I am always hesitant about societies with high ideals, for I first want to know if they act as well as talk. However, as soon as Dr. Murray introduced me to the Honorary Organiser of the Society, Lilian Hardern, that settled me. Anyone accustomed to evaluate people could see how Lilian was dedicated to her work. With an outstandingly good brain, capacity for quick reaction and sound judgment, she devotes herself night and day to solving the problems of individuals. Those in difficulty who apply to the Society can rest assured that their cases will have a full investigation and then, if justified, all help—as witness the Crichel Down case. Without the Society I doubt if the famous Enquiry would have been held. Moreover, victims of compulsory purchase by councils and victimised individuals are sustained as in the case of Douglas Rookes of the notable case of *Rookes v.*

Retirement

Barnard—the unfortunate draughtsman employee victimised by his union and allowed by the B.O.A.C. directors to be a scapegoat. Britain needs people with courage and a sense of responsibility who will fight bureaucratic control.

I am particularly interested in the Gabbitas-Thring Charitable Trust of which I have been Vice-Chairman under Sir Sydney Roberts, Vice-Chancellor of Cambridge University, since its inception in 1960. The managers of the Gabbitas-Thring company, Mr. R. W. Skene, Mr. G. M. F. Alston and Mr. P. H. Bromfield, with a great sense of responsibility and generous desire to help others, changed their famous educational agency into a trust in order that all money not required for upkeep, salary and wages should accumulate to provide Bursaries for the children of professional people. Preference was to be given to clergy and teachers to enable them to give their sons and daughters the type of education provided by Independent Schools. With present fees and cost of living this is frequently impossible in many professional families, without help of this kind. Considering the number of professional people who have come from rectories and vicarages and the contribution that they have made to English education over the centuries, this is indeed a worthy object. Often incumbents live far from a good day school and in any case they have too busy a life to provide a background for their children such as can be obtained in boarding schools. Also many have the affection for their own Public Schools and long for their sons to have the same advantage of first-class teaching and the widening of vision that can only be gained by the close companionship of a boarding school.

Each year a group of us, with Mr. Skene, see the applicants and award the bursaries. It was exciting when we could see the child as well, but with the price of fares on British Railways these days we do not insist on asking them to come from long distances and involve themselves in expensive return fares. Having all my life had contact with teachers, many of whom have been daughters of clergy and having the family back-

167

ground of clergy myself as well, I know full well what this financial help means to the whole family and I admire the imaginative outlook of the managers of this Trust. Since the sad death of Sir Sydney, we have been without a Chairman, but Lord Caccia, former diplomat and now Provost of Eton, after attending our last meeting, has promised to become our Chairman.

The European Union of Women, British Section, interests me greatly. Initiated by Alison Tennant through her hard work and enthusiasm it is doing good work through the medium of the commissions which visit the other branches in the various capitals of Europe and thus raises the prestige of Britain. Our British members of the Council of Europe confirm that its influence is great and helpful. The commissions are composed of Members of Parliament, local government officials and woman active in all branches of British life. My days of activity in such enterprises are over, but the Union needs the support of us older people to help with the annual Market and to raise funds to cover the travel expenses. I am only hoping that one day Spain, which I now know so well, will join, for then I can be of more help by way of translation and contacts with people in Madrid.

It will be evident that I have not lived an idle or a boring life, even though, as time has gone on, I have gradually had to limit my activities. As I have mentioned, we moved from Albert Hall Mansions towards the end of 1965. During the latter part of our time the rooms above us, which were built for maids—when such existed!—and for boxrooms, were let to residents. As our ceilings were not soundproof, the person above drove me nearly crazy with her loud T.V. The College of Science had been enlarged and spoilt our view which we both loved. The traffic had increased and was really tiresome. Most important of all, Maud, who had ceased bicycling at eighty, found the shops too far off. For almost two years we hunted for a flat; then I discovered that the Legal and General Assurance Company owned flats in Kensington and at once wrote to kind Mr. Kenneth

Adams, whom I had known of in Westonbirt days and who had been the saviour and guide of what was then called the Allied Schools. He put me in touch with their estate people and within a week we were viewing what is now our flat at 60 Stafford Court in Kensington High Street.

I at once fell in love with this room in which I now write. It is large, at the top of the building, with a glorious view over to the Surrey hills and with the sun streaming in all day as it faces south-south-west. There are two bedrooms, two sitting-rooms and, such a luxury, two bathrooms. All seemed so perfect, for we are over the shops and have our bedrooms over a silent courtyard so that we hear nothing at night.

All was well until it became obvious that Maud was getting very lame and the doctor pronounced that she had Parkinson's Disease. There was nothing for it but to find a home for her and what a problem that was! I should never have achieved it but for the help of Dame Dorothy Vaisey and Miss Herbertson of The Friends of the Poor and Gentlefolk's Help, who took Maud for a month at their nice home in Wimbledon, although unfortunately they could not fit her in for longer than that. However, now she is at the nursing home of the Holy Family at 20 Quex Road, N.W.6, where I visit her as often as possible. We are both independent and not the least alike and that has made life so easy. Maud has immense courage and now in the home she puts me to shame, for she puts up with all the loneliness this involves. I hate being without her and in particular having been the perfect secretary, discreet to the n'th degree, she had always known every problem and it was such a comfort to be able to discuss everything with her. After such companionship and sharing, this flat seems too empty now and my brain seems stultified for lack of someone to whom to express ideas. To part, after thirty-five years, is not easy, for we have always shared our views and everything.

I suppose old age has problems for most people. It makes me angry to hear this Government utter their sob stuff about widows. Why widows? Their husbands probably earned far more than professional women. If they have young children, they get family allowances for which we pay in taxes. If they have older ones, they have people who look after them. I think life is harder for spinsters.

CHAPTER ELEVEN

INDEPENDENT TELEVISION AUTHORITY

⌒⌒⌒

A T THE END of July 1954 I returned from one of my
Continental journeys rather hot, dirty and untidy. It
was 2 p.m. in the afternoon and I was unlocking my
front door when I heard the phone ringing. I went to pick up
the receiver and a male voice said, 'Is that Miss Popham?'

'Yes,' I replied. 'Who is speaking?'

The answer astounded me.

'I have been trying to get you for days. The Postmaster-
General wants to see you urgently; can you get to the G.P.O.
by 3 o'clock?'

'Whatever does he want?' I exclaimed. 'What have I done?
I am dirty and can't come at once as I am only just this minute
back from holiday.'

The voice replied: 'He wants to see you by 3 o'clock, so do
your best.'

I had a very hasty wash and hurried off in my Mini, much
wondering why Lord de la Warr wanted me. Owing to having
been abroad and not seen the English papers for months, I was
not even aware that Independent Television was coming about
so soon.

On my arrival, to my immense surprise, Lord de la Warr
asked me if I would like to be a member of the Independent
Television Authority. Naturally I was delighted, for I abominate
monopolies and was all for there being an independent television to create competition and consequently raise the standards of viewing. Not owning a T.V. set myself, I felt an

entirely inadequate person, but I accepted and asked who were the other members. Apparently, apart from Kenneth Clark, the Chairman, these were all appointed separately and none of us knew who the others were until we met on 4th August. I was pleased to find that I would be working under Kenneth Clark whom I knew so well. I had also once met Lord Layton and his wife, when she had lectured at Cheltenham. It was a privilege to be able to get to know them much better. I now saw a good deal of him and came to respect him very much, whether in connection with I.T.A. at his house or when he invited Maud and myself to see the results of the 1955 Election at a room in Grosvenor Street in company with himself and other distinguished people.

The Authority consisted of:
Sir Kenneth Clark, K.C.B. (Chairman)
Sir Charles Colston, C.B.E., M.C., D.C.M. (Vice-Chairman, September–December 1954)
Sir Ronald Matthews, J.P., D.L., M.Inst.T. (Vice-Chairman from December 1954)
Lord Aberdare of Duffryn, G.B.E. (Scotland)
Lt.-Col. Chichester (Northern Ireland)
Sir Henry Hinchliffe, J.P., D.L.
Dr. T. J. Honeyman, J.P. (Wales)
Lord Layton, C.H., C.B.E.
Miss Dilys Powell
Mr. Thorneycroft, C.B.E.
and myself.

Of these I was most delighted to see Dilys Powell for I shared with her her love of Greece and had read all her books, including *Coco*, whom I had met at her house, lovely poodle that he is. I very much admire her charm and her clear critical brain and likewise her knowledge of films which was such an asset to us.

The first meeting of the I.T.A. was in the Postmaster-General's offices: for we had nothing, no premises, staff, absolutely nothing until Kenneth Clark found some rooms in Wood's Mews off Park Lane, to be used for the time being, until better premises could be acquired.

It was very exciting to be in at the beginning of the new venture. After all the debates for and against, the immense amount in the press and the heated opinions expressed on every side, the desire of the public was granted; for the Conservatives, with their faith in free enterprise, won the day by a small margin and the Act was passed in March 1954 and became law on 30th July. The Authority was to correspond to the B.B.C. Board of Governors.

One occasion that stands out strongly in my memory was when Sir Henry Hinchliffe and I went together to the Distinguished Strangers' Gallery to hear a most exciting debate concerning Commercial Television which took place after it had been started for a short time. I had been fortunate enough to have two tickets given to me by Mrs. Morrison, wife of Mr. W. S. Morrison, the Speaker.

The first urgent problem for the Authority was to collect a nucleus of staff and above all to select a Director General. The number of prominent people who applied to be appointed to this responsible post was astounding. Out of the 332 applicants we were, I am convinced, right to appoint Sir Robert Fraser, then working on MI5. Sir Kenneth, who knew him, had asked him if he would care before making a decision to see Sir Charles Colston (who was Deputy Chairman from August to September 1954, when he was replaced by Sir Robert Matthews) and myself. Sir Charles invited me to lunch at his house in Albany; and there we saw Sir Robert and all lunched together. I had absolutely no doubt in my mind that he was the man for the job, which indeed has been proved by the fact that he is still the Director General. This clever Australian, with his background as Director General of the Central Office of Information, with his immense capacity for facing problems—weighing the pros and cons—and his friendliness and consideration for persons and policies, did invaluable work for the Authority, which was faced with 'building an edifice which corresponded to no known pattern'—I quote from the first Report.

This early period was one of intense activity and from the first we had numerous meetings from the days at the G.P.O., in Wood Mews, and when we moved into our first real house, 14 Princess Gate. The Authority had to conform with the clauses of the Act. The most important of these concerned balance and quality in the programmes, which meant that, whether in general entertainment, or for educational or other special purposes, it must appoint the right companies and rely upon them, while exercising a measure of supervision.

It became clear that the best way to ensure the accuracy and impartiality of the news was to have a special News Company that would cover the activities of all the contractors, and to appoint an Editor-in-Chief who would be responsible to the I.T.A. The companies' proposal of Mr. Aidan Crawley for this post was approved by the Authority.

I must not go into detail of the work undertaken by the Authority, which in any case can be found in all the Annual Reports presented to the Postmaster General each March, but I can say that under Sir Kenneth the meetings were of immense interest, everyone contributing according to their knowledge and understanding; while the technical side was worked out by Sir Robert and the technicians. The religious programmes, it was agreed, should be produced by our representatives on the Religious Committee of the B.B.C. under the Bishop of Bristol.

My own interests were largely in the religious and children's programmes, but I found the whole project intensely fascinating.

1955–56 was a year of great activity; programme contractors had already been appointed: Associated Television, Associated Rediffusion and Granada T.V. Network Ltd. Everything was most exciting and it is evidence of the enormous amount of work and enthusiasm of all the staff that an Authority, which began with absolutely nothing in August 1954, went on the air on

22nd September 1955, its coverage being then the whole of the London area.

It must have meant a tremendous strain for the Chairman, Director General and for the staff working closely under them to produce this miracle, for miracle it was in one short year to organise the Authority, build up a staff, decide the administrative, programme and commercial policies, select the contractors and get the transmitters constructed. The companies too had their work cut out, for they too had to obtain and train staff, build and equip studios and develop programmes. Then, for the I.T.A., advertisers had to be secured and the financial side settled, and there was still the problem of seeing that the advertisements complied with the rules laid down in the Act.

I remember the excitement of going to Croydon to see the first transmission from the mast there, and a few months later our expedition to Birmingham to see the Midlands first transmission. The Birmingham train journey stands out in my mind on account of our comic arrival at Snow Hill Station, when the stars for the entertainment had just arrived and all the porters had gone with them! Kenneth Clark saw a luggage barrow, took the suitcases belonging to Dilys and myself, amongst others, and solemnly wheeled them to the taxis— what a pity there was no photographer! It reminded me of a Cheltenham workman who had said to me of Lord Bessborough, 'He's a real gentleman; you know the real kind by the way they'll always do anything to help.'

The entertainment side was a new life to me. I remember clearly going to parties and T.V. shows at A.T.V. and Rediffusion, where one saw many people and found much of interest. One event that stands out was a luncheon at the American Embassy with T.V. personalities. I don't remember if it was Kenneth, or who it was in the Chair at the head table, but I know he had to propose the royal toast after the *soup*! It was supposed to be a formal lunch, but the Americans had started smoking and this was the only way to cover things up. Although we all cared tremendously for the things of serious importance,

I for one have to admit that I also found much enjoyment in the numerous parties and other functions that I attended.

During the year 1955–56 not only the London area with its huge population was provided with Independent Television coverage, but also the Midlands in February 1956 and the Lancashire area in May 1956, to be followed by a Yorkshire station in the autumn.

I had very much enjoyed my two years on the I.T.V., and in August 1956 Lord Layton, Lord Aberdare and I all left at the end of our appointments. No one could take part in the construction of an additional television without serious thought as to the effect it would have on the country as a whole. A medium that so powerfully enters the majority of homes is bound to have an influence for good or ill, and one prayed that it might be an influence for good. I say without hesitation that I.T.A. has always realised its responsibility and worked with this aim in mind.

I am convinced that the public should have the right to exercise its choice between programmes. Before the advent of I.T.V. this was not possible—it was a case of the B.B.C. only and take it or leave it. I am also convinced that the competition between the two raised the standards. Many do not believe this, for memories are short; but those who take the trouble to investigate the matter all come to the same conclusion.

On retirement from I.T.A., I did not lose my connection with the Authority, for I was appointed to the Children's Advisory Committee. For the first two years I worked under the Chairmanship of Mr. W. Hamilton, Head of Westminster School and then Rugby. Then there followed Sir John Wolfenden, and with both these men I had much in common.

When the Children's Committee was formed, one of my Old Girls, Janet Hills, had been appointed as Secretary and Adviser to the Committee and would with her clear critical brain and genuine care for individuals have been excellent, but an illness and her sudden death prevented her taking up the post. After much searching, Miss Jan Choyce was appointed and proved

9. The Independent Television Authority, 1955

to be a very pleasant person with whom to work; her being on
the British Board of Film Censors of films for children was a
great asset.

After the Authority I missed the sense of hard work and
solidarity. Mr. Jack Longland I found always interesting, and I
have often wished I should again meet Miss O'Connor, Mrs.
Neal and others who all worked so well as a committee.

During the meetings we had great discussions and Sir William
Alexander and Sir Robert Gould had a great deal to say, with
most of which I usually disagreed, as I still do now when I read
their views on education in the Press.

The committee had a number of problems to tackle, especially the means of presenting religion and the promotion of
education. Rediffusion came forward with the suggestion of
televising broadcasts to schools. This needed consultation with
other organisations and the company was directed to get into
personal touch with these. They did so with such success that
they were able, with the sanction of I.T.A., to start these broadcasts by May 1957. 'Westerns' were another problem. Personally I don't see why they should do harm, any more than the
reading of Ballantyne, Henty and other exciting authors harmed
us in our youth, for they are not the kind of things children can
copy—and are far removed from our English way of life. What
I do object to are all the films of fighting in streets and factories
and similar violence; all that may encourage theft and similar
crimes and are liable to arouse the wrong spirit in youthful
viewers and not a real sense of adventure.

The educational programmes were originally shown in the
London and Midland areas, and by 1957 in Scotland, too, when
two Scottish members were added to the committee. Miss
Choyce reported to us the content of the children's programmes
and the reactions. Our main object was to have entertainment
for the young of a kind that would open their eyes to the
wonders of the world and widen their vision, and we urged the
Companies to seek for fresh creative ideas. Arrangements were
made for previews of all these programmes and the Committee's

views were published in co-operation with research among groups of parents, on films with any content of aggression in them.

1958–59 was an important year, for in September a short report was published entitled 'Parents, Children and Television' and in December we and the Authority warmly welcomed the Nuffield 'Television and the Child'—a very careful and longer report on the effect of T.V. on children.

We still urged that there should be more drama with characters working out their problems by peaceful means rather than by violence. Associated Rediffusion produced good serial stories and an excellent magazine programme 'Let's Get Together', A.T.V. a good one on sports and hobbies and Granada did much to encourage natural history. We were all delighted when Mary Field was appointed by A.T.V. and A.B.C. as adviser on programmes for the young.

I ended my appointment in 1960. We had had on an average six long meetings a year and a great deal of work was done between them. I often wish that armchair critics could know the amount of careful thought and hard work that goes on in the background. It is so easy to sit back and condemn this or that without depth of thought or logic.

I believe only those who have been on the Authority itself can have a tiny glimpse of the gruelling work of the early days done by the Chairman and Director General and their staffs; and I know that the activity has continued under successive chairmen and Sir Robert Fraser.

For me, to be connected with the I.T.A. was a great and fascinating experience, for which I am grateful. It opened up a new life and I now follow the changes in T.V. with great interest. The work in many ways was closely connected with my lifelong interest—education, schools and young people.

CHAPTER TWELVE

INDIA AND OTHER TRAVELS

∞∞∞

I HAVE ALWAYS regarded it as one of the outstanding advantages of the profession that we have our holidays of varying length during which we are able to widen our range of experience by visiting other countries as time and occasion allows. During the course of my narrative I have given some account of my holiday excursions and in my retirement I found that I was not bound by the exigencies of term-time. However, I am aware that I am getting towards the end of my story and my publisher firmly reminds me that it would need another book to include everything which I wish to put in. Accordingly, I have to be content with this small number of vignettes concerning my more memorable journeys during my later years.

*　　*　　*　　*　　*

Long ago at Westfield I used to envy those who had seen India and I longed to go out East. However, as I have had to tell, my star led me to a Western Dominion rather than an Eastern one—and I hope that I have made it evident that I do not regret this for a moment. Always, however, I loved to have girls from India among my pupils, never thinking for a moment that I should ever go there for myself.

Then in the autumn of 1953 when, as I mentioned in my last chapter, Maud Kidney and I were in the throes of house-moving and I was embarking on plans to teach myself to type, my friends Krishna and Mohini Advani invited me to go, passage paid, to visit them in Bombay. The Advanis were exceptional people, as are their two daughters Shirin, who came to College, and Geetoo who, on my advice (as her parents had a flat in Curzon Place) went to the Frances Holland School whose Head was Margaret Bowden who had for sixteen years been an outstanding member of the C.L.C. staff. The Advanis often visited College when Shirin was there and I would visit them in London in return. They had travelled much and spent a great deal of time in the United States: Krishna and Mohini accordingly had all the best of East and West in them. They were, as I have said, exceptional people, not only on account of their considerable wealth, nor even their culture and width of vision, but also for the true and deep faith which they lived out in their lives.

Krishna was—and alas I have to say 'was', for it was a great tragedy when he was killed in the only one ever Air India disaster in Switzerland in January 1966—a person of immense integrity. He was head of the Bombay Stock Exchange and economic adviser to successive Maharajas of Nepal, a country where they had spent a considerable time owing to long visits to the Palace. At the same time Krishna devoted himself to the care of his family and all his own and Mohini's relations. When he gave up the stock exchange he dedicated himself to the building up of the industries of his own country for its general betterment and that of humanity. Although they are Hindus, I never felt entirely out of harmony with them for, as Mohini put it, 'We believe a God of Love made and directs us all.' They are the modern type of Hindu and though their religious services are so different from ours, yet they are still in harmony and when I attended one with Shirin who interpreted, I realised that we were all of us living by prayer to the one and only living God.

I suppose all those who have lived in and visited India have special visions that they will never lose. I certainly have. There was my first night when we drove in from the Bombay airport through the crowded streets where the heat beat up from the ground bringing with it the scent of mangoes, papyri and other products from the market. Then there was the beauty of the lights, 'Queen Victoria's Necklace', round the still, blue bay. However, it is always people and animals that interest me most and when I was up at early dawn I found it fascinating to watch from my window the men in their white dhotis talking away to each other in earnest discussion, as they sat refreshing themselves in the air on the sea wall. There was the quiet movement of people walking either barefoot or with sandals such as the Indian servants in the Advani household, gentle-voiced Joseph, Karumsi, Ayer and the rest. The peace and quiet both indoors and out gave an atmosphere of rest and meditation that was so different from our noisy London streets.

Then there was Agra with the Taj Mahal in the moonlight that took me back through the centuries and, ten miles away, Fatipur Sikri with its red sandstone buildings lightened by the endless number of green parakeets and the monkeys all along the road—small, anxious-looking ones, mothers with babies on their back, shy but brave enough to take from our hands all the nuts and fruit we had brought them.

Delhi brought me back again to modern life and politics. I was invited to visit Nehru at his house and I have to admit that I risked his hot temper when we started arguing and he seemed so completely unappreciative of all that the British Raj had done for India. I did feel, however, more *en rapport* with Vice-President Rhada Krishnan and I was deeply interested in all that he told me.

I still visualise the golden temple of the Sikhs at Amritsa not for its beauty but for its setting against the turbulent town where Indians and Pakistanis had fought against each other so cruelly. It was here that I saw a poor emaciated dog left to die in the gutter, and I was shocked when the chemist to whom I appealed for help was so reluctant to give me the chloroformed rag for which I asked with a view to giving this poor thing a peaceful end.

Aurungabad, on the other hand, stays in my mind for its

flowering trees and for the fact that from there we, the family, the servants and all of us, visited the caves of Ellora and Ajanta —those tremendous Jain and Buddhist carvings of the fourth– thirteenth centuries A.D., and the Kalaisa Temple hewn out of solid rock. I still dream of these, for their beauty gave me a sense of reverence and peace in that country of red dust and heat.

To me, to cross the Ganges with the great mobs along the riverside and to visit near Benares the bodhi tree under which they say the Lord Buddha sat, brought a different India to my mind. In Calcutta even the places of interest and the seething port did not eradicate a sense of evil, this in spite of much hospitality from English and Indian friends.

I dearly loved the south with the Mahabalipuram submerged temples near Madras and, in the depth of the inland country, the Nilghiri Hills with their tea and coffee estates. I was enchanted to find high up in the pinewoods great activity going on inasmuch as a house was being put up for the Queen to enable her to have a place to rest during her tour of India. Largeish monkeys swarmed around, calling from the trees, I am sure that the Queen and Prince Philip must have enjoyed them. These monkeys were dubious of us at first, but they soon came forward to hold my hand and eat bananas. When I read of the cruel transportation of monkeys to Europe and America for purposes of animal experimentation in our Western laboratories my blood boils and I think of all the ones with whom I made friends.

Also it enrages me to hear of elephants being killed for the sake of their tusks being removed for the ivory trade. Above all the other delights of the south, the elephant kedda was the most exciting. I can see them now, two large elephants carefully guiding a little one between them whilst other huge ones carried tree trunks on their tusks and the women fed the baby ones on balls of straw and honey. So trusting were they that one small one threw his trunk round my neck and another pressed against me, whilst the mother watched with a contented look on her face. Close to the nearby river, the bamboos made their brittle tinkling sound in the wind. I think that this was the highlight of my Indian visit, but I also enjoyed seeing the tea and coffee estates of Mysore and Bangalore with their fresh green and flame-coloured trees.

My deep interest in people gave my stay in Bangalore a special pleasure of its own, for it is the home of the various retired Nepalese maharajahs, very rich people of courtesy who gave simple entertainment in their lovely homes, treating one as an intimate friend. And what beautiful women the maharanis are!

Sometimes when I am half-asleep, I see too the high rock at Thirupparakundam near Bombay where daily a gentle priest, after having at noon put food before his god, awaits the punctual arrival at 12.5 of two huge white birds who come to be fed from his hand.

India and its people and its animals will remain ever in my heart and I give thanks for my friendship with the Advanis.

* * * * *

It was in 1947 before my retirement that Mr. Thynne Henderson and his Danish wife invited me to Stockholm where he was our minister. Helen and her three sisters from College had gone out for the summer holidays to what was their new home during the previous year and brought me back an invitation.

It was pleasant to be introduced to the people of this civilised and progressive country, but what struck me forcibly in 1947 was that the Swedes were still 'sitting on a fence' and one could sense this immediately when one met them. When I lunched for instance with Mr. Lönnroth, head of the Bank of Sweden, my first question to him was, 'On what side were the Swedes in their hearts, or haven't they any hearts?' He laughed and said, 'How wise I was to lunch you in a private room!'

Even after I had seen the Hendersons' cottage on Ingaro Island and their house near Nynäshamn, the old town of

Boring—Never!

Gamba Staden with its attractive restaurants, *The Golden Peace* and *Bellman's Ro*, both famous for Bellman and his drunken cronies, the old cobbled city and castle of Drottingholm, whilst admiring the beauty and cleanliness of everything, I still did not love Sweden. Perhaps, I thought, Upsala University will show me another side of their character. It surprised me by the fact that its academic life was so very different from that of our own Universities.

After a peaceful and happy holiday with all its hospitality, I returned glad to have seen Sweden, but totally out of sympathy with a nation that had refrained from taking part with all of us who fought for freedom against an evil aggressor.

* * * * *

In 1946 Mr. A. P. M. Orr, manager of J. P. Coats Ltd. for Southern Italy came to Cheltenham to enter his daughter, Marina, who was duly brought along later by his wife, Marta. She was a pretty, intelligent child of eleven who had been educated in Italy and then the Isle of Man where her mother had nursed during the war whilst Alex Orr was in the forces. Marta moved to London and we saw much of each other and were close friends until her tragic death in 1951. Of Central European extraction and brought up in Trieste, Marta Orr was a rare person, brilliant, spontaneous and full of courage. She spoke perfect Italian but did not know a word of English when, during the war, she had come to England with two small children and had to make herself understood. Her English pronunciation was often amusing; for instance, for 'pitch dark', she would say 'peach dark', but she became very fluent and indeed, with her vivacity, our language often seemed to take on new life and fresh meanings. She had no inhibitions and made friends with all classes.

I first visited them at Posilipo with its beautiful situation overlooking the Bay of Naples and quite near Herculaneum and Pompeii. I frequently visited these latter places and like-

184

wise it became my diversion to wander about Naples—where I found many friends, including those in Spaccanapoli (Street of Thieves) where I went to buy my Swiss Player's cigarettes. On my first visit the tobacconist took me on a short sightseeing tour to see all the lovely corners and vistas around. However, when I returned next year on the same errand for my cigarettes, he replied brusquely (although I thought that I detected a wink), 'No foreign cigarettes; go to the back of the queue.' Rather dismayed, I did as I was told, but when the rest of his customers had departed, he rushed at me, kissed me on both cheeks and said of course he had Player's, but there had been police spies in the queue whom he had to get rid of. I was then taken with great courtesy to meet his wife and family. Once before, on my first visit, I had asked a policeman where I could get cigarettes. He looked at his watch and replied, 'In three minutes I shall be gone and then you can ask one of the men standing over there.'

I was at first dismayed by some of the prices. In a shop that sold cardigans I asked the price: it was absurd. I declared, 'I am English, not American.' 'Oh,' replied the girl, 'just around the corner you will get the same as these for just half the price.'

Naples is a city of surprises. Alex Orr took me to visit Vincenzo Belli who with his large family conducted a wholesale business with a vast turnover, all in cash and with no apparent organisation. For this was the last stronghold in Italy where small traders could do a wholesale trade at the narrow margin of 1% to 3%.

There were always unexpected episodes. I was staying with the Orr family in a beautiful villa outside the town, scented with orange and lemon trees in the garden. One day I went for Marta to the village greengrocer. After serving me, the old woman said that the Pope had asked everyone to pray for the elections that were just due. Would I look after her shop for half an hour whilst she went to church? I did, but as nothing was priced clearly I just hoped that the customers were honest: they must have been, for the owner was quite content on her return. Alex always praised the Neapolitans for their honesty.

Another episode but a less pleasant one was when, on my way

to visit Annette Aprile, who at Cheltenham had taught me all the Italian I knew, and her mother and sister Lily, I saw a man beating his donkey cruelly. In fury I rushed at him, seized the cane and started to apply it to him. Within seconds there was a crowd gathered and an uproar. However, I did get his name and reported him to the Animal Welfare Society.

One day Marta and I crossed to glorious Capri with its Blue Grotto and saw Anacapri, made famous by that lover of animals, Dr. Axel Munthe. Another time Alex, always a generous host, took Marta and me across by boat to visit friends in Palermo before sending us on a trip round Sicily. Palermo with its famous Monastery of Monreal entranced me. We set off on our coach tour round the island with armed police riding in front and behind to protect us from the bandits. We had an amusing incident in Agrigento, where a room had been booked for us at 'the best hotel'—the most awful dump in which I've ever had to sleep. A little shopkeeper, whom Alex knew, met us to take us to see the sights—to his mind the most exciting one was a new and little-used railway station, but we, of course, were more interested in the Greek temple! Our sufferings in the hotel were compensated for by the almond blossom which that late spring was at its very best. After the Roman remains in Syracuse and a climb up the slopes of Etna I looked forward to our last port of call which was Taormina, a famous beauty spot. My interest was damped, however, owing to the fact that the picturesque town was occupied by endless Germans and, worst of all, a German had converted the lovely ancient monastery into a luxury hotel. Give me every time Palermo and Monreal!

My last two visits to the Orrs were following my retirement when I was most desperately missing dogs—for I had decided I could not keep any dog in a London flat. When Jester had died early in the war I replaced him by a bombed-out dog, whom I had obtained from the P.D.S.A.—a terrier puppy, Peter, found under a destroyed house. As I loved dogs far too much to keep one in the restricted life of a London flat, Peter, then nearly fifteen, stayed on in College with the Weaver family.

Spain

Imagine, therefore, my joy to find that Marta and Alex had two poodles who at once became my devoted friends.

These two were with them also the following year in Grignano near Trieste—where they occupied me during my stay in taking them for walks in the woods, throwing sticks and playing ball. I found the atmosphere around Trieste quite different from that at Naples. A curious sense of antagonism prevailed in many of the villages which were still peopled by Communists, although in Trieste itself the people were pleasant enough. The British Consul advised me not to enter Yugoslavia as I might be suspect, for the Communists still considered the Orrs Italians simply because they had lived and worked in Italy.

My only other visit to Italy was a joyous time in Rome with John and Janice da Silva when John was at the embassy. Janice, an Old Cheltonian and great friend of Aileen Dodds-Parker (*née* da Costa), was as ever full of life and delighted to take me over the Vatican City which I knew less than any other part of Rome. Leila May and Peter Partner were also there then and had collected other friends to meet me. Every time I go to Rome I long for a month to see classical Rome, another month for mediaeval Rome and nearly as long for modern Rome with its lovely spring flowers.

* * * * *

A visit to Spain with my friend Betty Amos has had a great influence on my years of retirement. Her husband Roy was head of a firm at Lloyds; and Betty and I had been friends since 1944 when they brought their Mary to College, where she was later deputy Senior Prefect before going on to read Classics at Cambridge.

In the Easter holidays of 1951 we flew to Madrid to have our first sight of the paintings in the Prado and of El Greco's works in the old city of Toledo. Visiting Walter Starkie, that great English Hispanophile, we obtained from him a glimpse of the wonders of Spain before we went south to Seville.

Boring—Never!

To me Andalucia is the most stimulating province in Spain with its excitable and courteous people. I am glad that I have seen so much of it before tourists poured in from all parts of the world. Who could go to Seville without being fascinated by its great dark cathedral, the immensely tall Giralda gleaming golden in the sun and offering to those who climb it a vision of beautiful scenery across the Guadalquiver—that waterway that has played so great a part in the history of Spain, and the Moorish Alcázar with its residence of princes. As I had an introduction to the Duchess of Alba, we called at her house on the outskirts of the city where, with typical Spanish courtesy, this tiny delicate-looking person met us in the large patio and took us to see over her house and have tea. Following this we took the train that wandered through Andalucia to Málaga and stayed in a hotel between that town and Gibraltar, where we met other friends and enjoyed the pinewoods. We visited the Rock itself. We enjoyed the Spanish folk of the countryside whose simple courtesy stemmed, I am sure, from training in both home and church. I left Spain determined, when the opportunity came, to learn the language and return.

My opportunity for this did not occur until in 1955 John and Margot Taylor returned from Mexico where he had been ambassador, to take up the directorship of Canning House, home of the Hispanic and Luso-Brazilian Councils. John soon invited me to join their Education Committee. Enjoying all the activities of Canning House and meeting the delightful social director, Marie Luisa Fordham, who is part Mexican and part British, I found that there were evening classes which I could join and it was at these that I learnt to love Spanish literature and history, and through friends there I was able to meet Spaniards themselves. The greatest joy of all was my introduction to Blanca Tomé de Lago. As she lives in Dolphin Square I see her more weeks than not and she teaches me to speak Spanish. I owe her much of the enjoyment of my retirement and in particular the fact that I can enjoy life when I go to Spain.

Spain

Since that time I have paid many further visits. Maud and I have visited Mallorca where we have English friends, and Teneriffe, that island of bananas, so perfect before it was occupied by German tourists in recent years, who are as unloved by the inhabitants as they are by us. Alas, we found ourselves unknowingly booked into a German-run hotel. Driving to it from the airport on our arrival, as we passed through the Otava Valley, gay with flowering trees and poinsettias, the taximan warned us about this and with appropriate gestures depicted to us the horrors that we were to experience. These were only too true and I found myself fighting the manager on the doorstep and throughout the five days which we had to stay there before we found vacant beds in a Spanish hotel. I hardly need say that I made many friends amongst the local population—the man who kept the leather shop and fiercely refused to mend a German suitcase, but, the German gone, said of course he would mend a British one. He would not work for pigs! The policeman in the central square was equally eloquent! When I asked him for the best hairdresser he unhooked his telephone from a tree and made me an appointment, explaining fiercely that I was English and not to be attended by the German assistant. How friendly all the natives were, the policeman remarking to me next day, 'Yes, your hair is good.'

The Spanish hotel on the heights above the town was gay and full of friendly people. We met a brave Canadian tied to a bath-chair, who has kept in touch with us ever since. How we enjoyed the beauty of the drive up Mount Teide, from which we could see every part of the colourful island, the 3,000-year-old Dragon Tree at Icod, and the botanical gardens with trees, plants and monkeys, and the unusual fishing boats in the bay.

From then on we concentrated on the mainland—Barcelona with its cathedral, the Ramblas filled with flower stalls, the ancient town hall and Bishop's palace, and above it in the Pyrenees the old Monastery of Montserrat.

Malaga—so Andaluz—a perfect spot in winter with its old streets, narrow and with the signs of bygone centuries and the

Boring—Never!

Casa de Cultura where I went to some lectures and ended by being asked to give a public lecture on English public schools, is a place one can return to frequently. The inhabitants, both English and Spanish, are *so* friendly, and it was not a bad idea for us to combine a visit there with one to old friends in Gibraltar, especially the Prossers. He has for years been Head of Brympton School and they always collected for us Cheltonians as well as their own friends. I wonder what they have suffered by Wilson's tactless dealings with Franco?

At Easter Valencia enchanted us with its beauties, especially the Lonja de la Seda—Gothic and still a stock exchange, but not only dealing in silk; also the cathedral and market square ablaze with carnations. When we went to a florist to get carnations at twopence a dozen to bring home, the saleswoman dived for a letter from America which she wanted translated into Spanish. I did this for her, and upon opening our boxes of flowers in England I found she had put in more than we had ordered, and orange blossom too. So it would appear that this historic city still preserves the generous spirit of the days of El Cid.

Once we went to Alicante, but none of that coast held attractions. We only have to thank it for the fact that we met there the manageress of the Richmond Hotel in Madrid, where afterwards with Maud and other friends I shared a flat in the hotel. Since then I have visited Madrid at various times, for I have many friends there and nearby; in fact I now stay with two of them as a P.G.

Such amusing things happen in Madrid. There are rules that one may not cross the road unless the signs permit. One day there simply was no traffic coming down the Alcalá, so I decided to run: and ran straight into the arms of a policeman! As I happened to be wearing a cherry-coloured coat, he greeted me with, 'Señora, your coat is very pretty, but you must not use it to stop the traffic!' Another day, a large dog stood by me and wanted to cross, so I held him by the collar and we crossed together. I stopped a policeman nearby and asked him if he knew where the dog belonged. 'No, Señora, isn't he yours?' 'No, he just asked to be helped to cross safely.' 'Are you British?' he asked. 'Yes,' I said. 'I suppose that is why he didn't bite you!' 'I never thought he would, but you think the British are mad, I suppose?' He roared with laughter and said, 'I should have expected him to.' I replied, saying, 'Stroke him and then he can ask you for help next time.' His face was a study but he did stroke him! Then I followed the dog to be sure he got safely to his home, and on arrival his mistress greeted him. She was a funny old woman who evidently was kind to him, but had never heard of putting his name and address on a disk. When I suggested it she just chuckled, but she did invite me into her small, but spotlessly clean basement room.

Then my taximen friends, too, are delightful. Last year one chased after me in his taxi and waved to stop me. 'Señora, two years ago I took you to Hotel Mercator and told you about my son in England, and you saw him and he came to see me. Oh! I was so glad, but I don't like his English wife. They are both common now and my son has not the pride we have. They have money. I say he's no good with money now he has lost his dignity and his religion. But I'm so glad to see for myself he won't go in for crimes like English people.' All this in a very busy street! Then he asked where I was going and took me, all the time pouring forth volumes about the awful English tourists with money but no manners. If only English tourists like the ones he talked of could realise the harm they do to Britain!

Typically, having taken me to the shop I wanted, he waited and brought me back and utterly refused to let me pay. 'No, Señora, you got my son to visit me. No, no, I've not lost my pride.'

Now that I know Segovia, Avila and much of Castile, as well as the magnificent *parador* at León and its cathedral with the old French glass, Salamanca with its superb Plaza Major and the University famous for Unamuno, Spain to me is almost my second home.

I was delighted when in 1962 I was asked to take a party of

the Schoolmasters' Wine Club, and in 1964 a party of doctors and their wives to visit the wine centres. Both trips were the greatest fun and everyone was fascinated by the beauty spots of Spain and exhilarated with the bountiful hospitality of the vintners.

I knew Spain well enough to know that, having flown to Madrid, we must go in a coach of the Marsans Agency, for their coaches are comfortable, their drivers excellent and experienced in touring on all the routes we went. The point of both trips was to combine the visits to the wine centres with those to the famous cities, and I arranged to alternate these. From Madrid we went direct to Toledo where everyone was entranced by El Greco, the silver makers and the historic Alcázar. On to the wines of Valdepeñas where Don Sanchez Gomez displayed his bodegas and gave lavish entertainment. Through Don Quixote's country with the windmills to Cordoba. Cordoba with its unique *mezquita* (mosque) to my mind is one of the most lovely and historic places. There, having friends in John Haycraft's Academia Britanica, I found someone willing to tour the party to the most lovely patios and all places of interest. After Montilla and Moriles, where the Alvears have stored their wine since 1729, a drive on one tour to the famous Nerja Caves and Malaga, before Granada with its Alhambra and Generalife and then to Seville, before going to Jerez, the sherry centre, where I knew most of the famous families, such as Beltran Dumecq and his wife Anne (*née* Williams), a Westonbirt pupil of my time there. The marriage had united the two great firms of William & Humbert with the Dumecq vintners. Our entertainment by these friends and Don Francisco de la Riva and Don Miguel Valdespino, and the invitation of Anne's cousin, Dagma, Marquesa de Tamerón, to visit her famous (but seldom seen by tourists) castle at Arcos de la Frontera, was a highlight. Exciting excavations enthralled the history lovers and all the archaeologists. The doctors' tour being a little longer than the others it was possible to return to Madrid via the old historic towns of Extramadura—Mérida, where every tower was inhabited by storks, and Trujillo, famous for its association with the Conquistadores.

One year Carol Plunkett, a member of the C.L.C. staff, and I went on a tour of Portugal where we rejoiced in the beautiful sights of Sintra and Coimbra University. We spent several delightful days with Mr. and Mrs. Windsor at Oporto, but we hurried on to our main objective which was in Spain—Santiago de Compostela in Galicia. So wonderful a city that it was worth the eleven-hour train journey of 120 miles from Viana de Castelo! Much as we loved the joyous freedom of the Spanish after the more dour and silent Portuguese, it was rather too much for us to have, on a boiling afternoon, all air obstructed by a Spaniard with an enormous guitar and endless young Spanish girls and boys clustering to hear him. But every annoyance vanished at the sight of the wondrous square of Santiago with its superb cathedral and the Hostal of Fernando and Isabela, Los Reyes Catolicos. Five days of perfect bliss, in a city whose beauty exceeds Venice in my eyes, gave me something unforgettable—a spirit of religion deep and true, beauty beyond belief, unique architecture, everything imbued with the history of the past passing on to the present courage and high ideals.

EPILOGUE

'T'ISN'T LIFE that matters, t'is the courage you bring to it.'
I read these first words of Hugh Walpole's *Fortitude* in
1914. They impressed me deeply then, and have lived in
my mind ever since. I am convinced that faith and courage
form the basis of a sound life.

As I come to the end of my memoirs my mind goes back to a
childhood spent in a home of perfect harmony and with a strong
sense of gratitude to parents who remained in love with each
other to the end. I never heard a quarrel between them nor even
a strong disagreement. Religion was seldom talked about, it was
lived and taught by example. Far from taking me to church too
young, my father said I must be old enough to understand that
to go into God's House was a privilege.

Some parents say they give no Christian teaching to their
children because they want to leave them to choose later. How
wrong! Surely parents should provide the basis for choice.
Children brought up with good Christian teaching may tend
to take much for granted, but later on if they begin to doubt
they can question from knowledge and find out how far they
can accept the truths they have been taught.

I went through this stage of doubt at Westfield; there could
have been no better place to enable me to surmount it. I passed
from blind acceptance to deeper understanding based on study
and logical thought. Without this experience I doubt if I could
have taught Scripture or indeed worked out the problems of
others with sincerity.

Epilogue

I am sure this experience helped me to help my pupils. I, in turn, introduced them to the writings of Archbishop Temple, Canon Quick, C. S. Lewis and Dorothy Sayers and other good writers on religious subjects. I was able to pass on what I had learnt—that peace of mind and courage to face life comes from faith: not a blind faith or ignorant belief, but faith that is reasoned, which leaps beyond reason to trust in God. There were many times in my life when my courage would have failed me had I not remembered, 'Not I, but Christ in me.'

Confident of God's help, I was able to deal with the problems, sorrows and questioning of those under my care. Because I loved teaching I never sought appointment as headmistress: I merely 'followed the star'. I loved teaching for itself. Always deeply conscious of my own inadequacy I was, however, inwardly aware that with each fresh responsibility I undertook I could count on God's help. I was confident of His guidance.

Old Cheltonians now married and with families, who often come to see me, remind me of the help they derived from College—'Do you remember that you were a fanatic for good scholarly work?' said one. She went on to say that, after being angry and resentful because I had called her shoddy and shiftless and had warned her that she was jeopardising her future, she had made up her mind to maintain proper standards and show me she could do this by her University results. 'Now,' she said, 'it has become a habit, and we have jolly well instilled it into our family.'

Another said the emphasis on deportment and courtesy had been invaluable, another that she had been imbued with a zest for living because she had been taught to put enthusiasm into her studies and indeed into all she did. 'Life,' she said, 'was full of interest and therefore happy.' She added, 'It still is, though it's pretty hard work.'

The variety of subjects we discuss is endless, it can be religion, a sense of service, a search for knowledge . . . many of them tease me about my admiration for Churchill—and above all they praise the teaching staff.

Boring—Never!

They remember the religious spirit which permeated College, the dedication of the staff . . .

How right this was! It grieves me to read so many appeals concerned solely with raising salaries in order to recruit more teachers. Whilst I am naturally anxious that teachers should be better paid, I am also sure that only men and women with a sense of vocation should go into the teaching profession. Inspiration to this end is needed. To devote one's life to the upbringing of the next generation is surely the best form of social service? Our country needs good teachers of all subjects to help improve the standards, to awaken intellectual curiosity and understand the needs of each child. This need ranges from kindergarten up and through the universities, and not only for academic subjects but for art, music and physical training.

I remember so well how much my girls gained, not only from the teaching of academic subjects, but also from dancing lessons, a training in free movement. How well I recall the way Madame Perigal, by her teaching of fencing, produced poise and thereby self-respect. Our fine art masters and mistresses not only discovered potential artists such as Moyra Jacobs, Brigid Reilly and Penelope Makins, but gave a sense of colour and beauty to many who later applied this to dress design and interior decorating. This sense of beauty added, too, to an appreciation of all that is best in nature, films, plays, art galleries and architecture.

Education without discipline is unworthy of that name, for this is the prelude to self-discipline. Oliver Stanley, that great Minister of Education, said that our country needs all kinds of schools, including Independent Public Schools with their fine tradition of learning and service. There must be scope for freedom of choice and adventure in education. The British people have always been courageous, liberty-loving individuals. The tumultuous welcome given to Sir Francis Chichester surely implies that the same spirit is alive today? If this is so it should be encouraged rather than the fostering of the Welfare State attitude—a 'get everything for nothing attitude'—which crushes ambition and accounts for the bad workmanship and apathy so prevalent at the present time. If Britain's influence in the world is to be restored, our leaders need to inspire every single person with a proper pride in his work. Initiative should be rewarded and sloth should go unrewarded. Then perhaps our exports would be a visible evidence abroad of our high standards, which they are not today.

Inspiration, not dictatorship, is needed and a clearer attitude to right and wrong. Maybe there would then be less talk of the Permissive Society, less pornography, perversion and 'pot'. It is sad to see on T.V. the 'hippies' depicted as living a life based entirely on emotion and self-indulgence. I heard one girl say that she despised all older people and had no use for her parents, yet added, 'no one should hurt other people'! Others said they were happy with their drugs and dreams. No thought of service to humanity, or realisation that they were destroying the best in themselves. It would seem that they despise the principles which have stood our country in good stead in all the crises of our history.

I wish the programme producers—especially those on the B.B.C.—had a greater sense of responsibility in the control they have over the important medium of television with its vital influence over the thought and outlook of viewers.

Do they not consider that the featuring of drug addicts and of groups who have allowed themselves to be associated with this cult can have a demoralising effect by giving the impression that these people are to be imitated by all those who wish to move with the times? Visitors from overseas comment on the fact that, until they have been here for a considerable time and have met a number of sane young people, they get a wrong idea of Britain. The emphasis on these freaks gives many of our weaker brethren the idea that by being normal happy citizens at home and at work they are being 'square' and 'not with it'. This may be good television, but it is a corrupting influence on society.

At the same time so anxious is the producer to use his 'stars' that frequently those who have something to say are excluded and there is lack of balance in the programmes. Worthless people are given prominence; worthwhile people are ignored. The persistent display of the sordid side of life quite outweighs the normal, the helpful, the educative and the constructive. There is a wrong attitude to contentious problems. For instance, in comment on the question of immigration any slight denigration of coloured people is 'news', while the immense tolerance of our home population is ignored. Even that customarily very good I.T.V. programme 'Three After Six' is occasionally spoilt by the speakers being chosen for their 'television image' rather than for their knowledge and experience of the subject under discussion.

Britain deserves, and indeed we must have, producers of greater depth, width of vision and freedom from bias.

A few days ago I watched a woman collect over a pound's worth of periodicals from a Tube bookstall. She and I were the only people on the station. We started talking and she told me that she lived in a council house with her husband, two sons and a daughter. She readily admitted that she had never considered the harmful effect on her family of reading sensational and trashy papers.

One theme has been running through my mind whilst I have been writing this book. It is the importance of the individual and the need for everyone to develop a sense of duty rather than rights. It is for this reason that I consider the time has come for all of us who care for standards and values to follow Viscount Bruce's advice. I well remember in 1951 when he came to speak at College, this great Australian urged that in peace-time we must not forget our imperial heritage. He talked of Britain's influence in the past and gave a great challenge to the generation to whom he was speaking. He said that for the sake of the whole world we must believe in ourselves, and to the girls he urged for the sake of the next generation you must 'Have faith and be prepared to fight for those things in which you believe, fight and fight to the last ditch: never give up fighting'. Then he quoted:

Epilogue

'Pray God our greatness may not fail
Through craven fear of being great.'

Now we have no Empire; the Commonwealth is dwindling; sanctions are used instead of statesmanship; patriotism is a 'dirty' word. We cease to defend those who have been our friends overseas and who have relied on us, in order to give priority, not always needed, to the social services at home. I heard another prominent Australian say the other day that he regretted the unwillingness of the British people to give of their best. He deplored our over-indulgent Welfare State. The next day the Government raised the Family Allowances!

I believe there are many who deplore these tendencies, yet few have the courage to say so. They strike one attitude in private and another in public in case they are considered 'square'. Yet there are those with courage. Miss Alice Bacon's fearless attack on drug-taking is to be admired. Her erstwhile political opponent, Dame Pat Hornsby-Smith, lost no time in endorsing her views. I, too, had read the issue of the *Queen* from which she quoted. It had left me wondering. Do we, I pondered, need to give so much publicity to the philosophy or daily habits of those who rely on drugs for their adventure? Perhaps it is our fault, sensation makes good news—good television—the public gets what it wants? But not what it needs.

Even Billy Graham said on leaving England recently, 'Unless we have a revival of religion and morals we are heading for some form of dictatorship in Britain and the United States.'

There are encouraging signs, however. One of these is the steady growth of the ecumenical movement. It will take much time and thought to bring all sections of Christians together, but Anglicans and Roman Catholics and the Greek Orthodox Church are at least talking to each other. Bishop Headlam did much to bring harmony between ourselves and the Greek Orthodox Church. The Pope is endeavouring to encourage contacts and to create an atmosphere in which unity is possible. There is a great deal of goodwill between the Anglicans and

199

the Free Churches. A united Christendom should do much to overcome the prevalent materialism and hostility to religion and to restore in our society our awareness of the supreme value of the individual.

Possibly I shall be thought 'square' to propound a Christian solution to our problems, but no one should ignore too readily the effect of two thousand years of Christian teaching as a civilising influence.

I am convinced that the most important factor in restoring the greatness of our country is the building of our homes on a Christian basis. What an influence this can have! Even in Russia, during a period of militant Communism, two men of great importance, Captain Nikolai Khokhlov in 1954 and Boydan Stashynsky, an officer of similar rank, in 1961, defected to the West purely owing to the influence of their Christian wives. If, in a Communist community, the influence of Christian women could persuade their men to incur such personal risks, while undergoing similar risks themselves, surely here in Britain Christian parents can afford to take a bold attitude, ignore the prevalent depression imposed by this period of decadence and devote themselves to instilling high principles into the rising generation.

The responsibility for progress rests squarely on each one of us. We have a duty towards the next generation. We must seek to understand them. Let us ask ourselves why they are choosing to abandon standards we have set. Sympathy, understanding, common sense and discipline in the early years will in the end, I am sure, reap a rich reward. The unalterable truths will survive.

★ ★ ★ ★ ★

Perhaps in conclusion I should give the explanation of the title I have chosen. Friends and parents would often say to me, 'You are a person of so many interests. Don't you find school life boring?' My answer was, 'Never.' It has been a life of hard

Epilogue

work from early morning to last thing at night: a life full of problems, decisions, anxieties and plans, but always there were vast numbers of individuals for whom one cared. The young have such a zest for life and are so full of life and laughter it would have been odd indeed had I not somehow been riding the waves with them. Life was indeed 'Boring—Never!'

September, 1967

AS OTHERS SEE US

HER YEARS AT WESTONBIRT

by Joy Burden (*née* Dickinson)

∞∞∞

WHEN MISS POPHAM came to Westonbirt we were agog. Would a tidal wave of innovations sweep the establishment? Life could be made mundane, if not hideous, by ridiculous rules; Mrs. Craufurd had scorned to use them. Her successor might reduce ours to the level of an 'ordinary school'. My own yardstick and authority on these was Angela Brazil, whose books had been an earlier addiction.

Changes came, but almost casually at first. We weren't weaned from 'Taps' the Guide chant, which had always been sung at bedtime, a link with Mrs. Craufurd's own Guiding days in Scotland. 'Taps' remained throughout my time, but was chanted before supper ere long, and became part of a wider paean of praise and recollection. We began calling it Vespers, simply because our new headmistress did. A grey Grecian robe vanished, the Greek movements apparently being fluid enough in other garb, and parents had cause for gratitude! Red berets, aired only in following the chase twice yearly, also faded with other unnecessary plumage.

Where Angela Brazil's headmistresses had introduced an impressive number of rules, 'Pop', which she was from the first (and never 'Pops'), presented personalities instead, by bringing a few pupils from her previous domain. We crudely dubbed them her Jersey Cows, and didn't want them to 'sell' the Channel Isles to us! Tactfully they refrained, but they certainly helped set a new academic pace. This didn't altogether impress, but the fact that they were quick to appreciate Westonbirt and its minions assuredly did; they were obviously a pedigree herd.

Miss Popham's own appearance was scarcely in the Angela Brazil tradition:

'Not very tall, slight, erect and elegant with prematurely grey hair (at least we weren't responsible for that!) and always well dressed. Her piercing blue eyes possessed an unusual brilliance when she smiled.' And parents, too, fell under the spell of that dazzling gaze, particularly the fathers!

This description, given by Muriel Corby, a former head girl, is reminiscent of the chatelaine of a stately home, which of course Pop was. She enabled Westonbirt to retain some of the fragrance of a great country house, even if its guests now came to stay for longer than in the days of the Holfords! Her predecessor had ensconced housemistresses in drawing-rooms, and to these we repaired in the evenings. Miss Popham, too, welcomed individuals and small groups to her sitting-room any hour of the day or night, God and work willing. No appointments made through secretaries preceded these visits, for those might have deterred the timid.

Like any redoubtable hostess of the Edwardian era she drew men of letters, wives of cabinet ministers, distinguished people from abroad and others who had made their mark in humble as well as exalted spheres. That they were so ready to regale mere schoolgirls with their experiences was a delightful tribute to the rising generation, but even more to the persuasive powers of Pop. She had a flair for stimulating brilliant conversation in the erudite, and a zestful response from the immature, perhaps one of her richer gifts.

Through her vision and diverse sympathies horizons could expand. In an apparently isolated rural environment the world, great causes and opportunities beckoned, unaided as yet by television. The staff caught the infection too. My own housemistress, Katharine Bevan, after seven years of us, took a slow boat to Japan, and had the holiday of a lifetime. Miss Godley and Miss Neville-Rolfe, inspired by Miss Popham's 'brainchild', the House of Citizenship, created ones of their own, and to these the young still flock. Miss Neville-Rolfe now combines

hers with secretarial training at Hartwell House, Buckingham-
shire, and her colleague runs delightful 'Look and Learn'
courses at Kingham in Oxfordshire, and in London too, where
students take a panoramic view of the twentieth-century world
and gain immeasurably thereby.

The glories of an English country house did not exactly
envelop us, but formed a backcloth to the sterner purpose of our
lives within it. Parkland and splendidly landscaped gardens
were ours to roam in, drawing, dancing, music and art were
there to enjoy. The library became what libraries have always
been to houses like these, and Pop's devotion to animals seemed
all of a piece. Whilst it in no way diminished her affection for
two-legged creatures, it jostled for position in Morning Prayers,
and her dogs were regular churchgoers too! In fact they escorted
her on most ceremonial occasions and remained discreet, but
reassuring onlookers during interviews momentous and otherwise. There was a certain feeling of luxury in those days, despite
bare corridors and lacrosse sticks hanging where hunting prints
might have reposed of yore. Miss Irby, now Mrs. Chamberlin,
conjectures: 'I wonder whether there was anywhere else where
one was met in a Daimler by a chauffeur at Kemble, not even
Tetbury, when one was a junior member of staff? It was still
the days of a chauffeurs' tent at Speech Day.'

If Mrs. Craufurd had been something of a *grande dame* the
next chatelaine was no less so, even if she had teaching in the
blood, and saw a wide cultural background married to highly
powered educational pursuits as a grand alliance and our
natural heritage. We didn't invariably share that vision, of
course! Tenacity in studies was expected of everyone, and our
days moved to a more swinging academic tempo with the
coming of Pop. We might be pavilioned in splendour, but we
had to acquire intellectual disciplines, and these by concentrated, sustained effort.

At her last Speech Day at Westonbirt, Miss Popham observed:
'We must teach the growing girl to tackle the problems of life
by scientific methods, careful observation, clear deduction and

accurate statement of facts.' She went on to mention that the Government by its recent enquiry into a Budget leakage had set an example which she considered educationalists must follow of demanding high standards of accuracy of thought and speech, which she declared were the outcome of the integrity of character for which the Empire had always stood. Miss Popham, whose politics were as blue as her eyes, presumably expected in the government of the day something of the quality of Caesar's wife!

Careful thought and courageous speech she applauded, but laziness was deplored. Once a child submitted poor homework, and upon being reprimanded told Miss Popham, 'I sort of thought I knew it vaguely.' This excuse carried no weight. Another explanation excited equal dismay. She was talking to a girl about something in itself quite unimportant. 'The entire school does it,' the fourteen-year-old informed her. Pop questioned this. 'Well, hundreds say they do.' Further investigation revealed that three girls said they did; two actually did. It was recognised that there was no desire to deceive, merely inaccuracy, but that was enough, and they provided two classical examples to quote afterwards with rueful humour.

Miss Popham was a past-master of the crisp deflating phrase. Yet she did not bear umbrage, and never harangued. Courteous in almost every circumstance herself, good manners were taken for granted; deviations from these were not. 'Indeed?' was sometimes sufficient rebuke. Dirty shoes worn in the vicinity of her drawing-room chair might provoke a quiet, 'Must you?' accompanied by a sweeping glance downward. 'It does not make one iota of difference,' brought some altercations to an astringent close.

Miss Popham was a crusader. Certain causes impelled unflagging allegiance, and her convictions shone through her life at Westonbirt. One of these focussed on international peace. Eminent men and women, members of the staff among them, spoke plainly about the state of the world, and often current affairs sessions kept mistresses and the upper school in no doubt that sinister forces were already threatening England's future security, and that of Europe and the world. Pop, ardent, although not fanatical, in the cause of freedom and the means of preserving it, radiated in her own attitude and outlook ideals which inspired not only the youth of the period, but countless adults who believed they had discerned in the aftermath of war, promise of peace for all time. As far as she was concerned there could be no let up, no ceasing from mental fight, nor leaving a stone unturned, let alone a sword resting idly in one's hand, till at least a few bricks of Jerusalem had been laid in the green and pleasant land around her. We sang Blake's 'Jerusalem', our school song, with a fervour almost amounting to a vow (at least some of us did!) and for me it still epitomises the spirit of Pop, and the mood of those days. It bred in me a lofty resolve to go out into the world anon and contribute a fragment to the growth of that New Jerusalem somewhere, sometime. But for our generation the way ahead was to be more militant, and destructive.

Rosemary Meynell divined this, and for her some of the hymn singing, though magnificent, was misdirected. She vehemently disagreed with Miss Popham, but they are still in friendly touch today, for both admire those who stick to their guns out of genuine conviction courageously upheld. Rosemary remembers:

'. . . In that tremendous hymn "Mine Eyes have seen the glory of the coming of the Lord" we were told that we must no longer sing "Let us die to make men free"—dying for one's country was then not quite the thing. "We must live to make men free . . ." was decreed, for this was the age of the Peace Pledge Unions. Efforts were made to recruit us all into the League of Nations Union. Since leaving school, my politics have moved steadily to the Left but, in those days, I was very Right Wing and even had some admiration for Hitler. Looking back, I see that Miss Popham represented liberal intellectual opinion of the time and that I was a black reactionary, but we were less than a decade away from the

outbreak of war in which we should all be asked to risk dying
to make men free; and some of us felt that the pacificism, so
popular everywhere that by-elections were being won on the
slogan "SCHOLARSHIPS NOT BATTLESHIPS", was leaving us
dangerously weak as a nation.

'Miss Popham never resented that, at the age of sixteen, I
helped to lead a faction in the school that opposed the
League of Nations Union brand of thought. I was allowed
to say my piece at debates, and the gentle and sincere Janet
Hills was well able to put the other point of view.'

Rosemary also recalls the impact of Pop upon herself and
some of her friends during the former's first year at Westonbirt,
and again this was refreshingly different to the impressions of
others resurrected after a gap of several decades! She writes:

'I was fourteen when Miss Popham arrived and I had
already been more than three years in the school. Like the
Rock of Gibraltar, Mrs. Craufurd had seemed an immovable permanency and the change of headmistress was a shock
to our youthful sensibilities.

'I had never met anyone like Miss Popham before. Like a
tiny glittering star she soon dominated our horizon.

'In the remaining years of my school life she was to teach
me how power and people can be handled, I almost said
manipulated but I do not wish to imply that she managed
the governors, parents, staff and girls for sinister ends. In fact
she saved the school from growing into a mere fashionable
resort for young ladies. Not that it had been that before, but
it was growing in that direction.

'Miss Popham made few changes her first term. She con-
ciliated and charmed those who remained from the former
régime and many who had proposed to leave decided to stay,
while the hard core who still had to work out their term's
notice before leaving found things going on as before. Then
things began to change rapidly. The teaching had not been
bad before. There had been women on the staff with the

capacity for awakening in the young a love of learning for its own sake. For better or worse they had been individualists. Now came a sterner régime, an emphasis on the passing of exams. Scripture had been taught by Miss Wace in a way that brought Bible stories to life and gave them a personal religious significance, but Miss Popham's Scripture pupils found themselves obliged to learn the dates and order of the Israelite Kings. The Rev. George Timins preached simple, comforting sermons that we had all loved, Miss Popham's evangelical approach was more militant. It was an intellectual rather than an emotional approach.

'When I moved into my last year at school Miss Popham did not encourage me to stay—I was not the stuff of which university scholars are made. I should *never* learn the dates of the Israelite Kings, though the story of Uriah the Hittite would always move me to tears by its tremendous poetry.

'So I left and moved out into the world of wage earning, a very cut-throat world which I would have been less equipped to cope with without what I had learned from Miss Popham. She had shown me the difference between the intellect and the emotions and let me see that she was capable of both. She had shown me the use of the iron hand in the velvet glove, how femininity can be used to disguise great strength of purpose and how, if you cannot bend people to your will, you must attempt to charm them.'

Pop knew, as many of her pupils were to discover in their own experience, that in certain situations only charm could win the day. Its infiltration into some areas of controversy might denote a crafty weapon, but in others it was more of a healing balm to be applied in deep sincerity. That, I believe, was her way. She could not have envisaged then just how closely most of us were destined to work with men on barrage balloon and bomb-site, in administrative post, hospital, camp and other arenas of war, yet she was, in effect, training us in good relationships with others anywhere. Pupils being prepared for the professions, for public life and marriage would soon be pouring into the services, the Admiralty, the Foreign Office and Red Cross. Some would pass right across and beyond the frontier of this world; two, in fact, were killed flying and one by shipwreck. Many were already married by 1939, and for them, too, the character training and help at various levels received from Pop and her staff was an equally valuable preparation for a war-time wife and mother likely to lose her husband on and off for the duration, and sometimes altogether. Like a few of her contemporaries in battledress, she might lack paper qualifications, but not the will to take responsibility and to slog it out. Legions of us (how Pop would deplore such imprecision!) found our former headmistress, long since established at the Ladies' College, Cheltenham, ready to give assistance and reassurance by written testimonials, personal consultations and cheering letters, no doubt by her prayers too, for Old Girls facing opportunities and problems of every kind.

Whilst we were with her, however, it was in personal encounter, and not on a platform that Miss Popham's influence permeated deepest and those drawn to her by distress found a life-line. One of these recalls:

'She and I started our Westonbirt life simultaneously. During this time I came to know her well, and became extremely fond of her because she gave me a great deal of help and affection during the first serious emotional crisis of my life. When I was thirteen, my parents separated (temporarily as it turned out, but no one knew this at the time). My father, whom I adored, departed overseas, whence he wrote me harrowing letters. Other sections of the family did the same, and I was torn with misery and conflicting loyalties. This now seems to me rather like an episode from an Evelyn Waugh novel, but at the time it was devastating. I've never ceased to feel gratitude and affection for Pop for her understanding. She had, and I expect still has, a very warm-hearted nature towards those she liked, which wasn't everyone! She was always available for me to go and see her, and point out my worries and problems to her. I honestly don't know what I would have done without her at this time and her good sense and sympathy. She had a way of treating me as an equal and not a child, which was a revelation to me of what an adult human being could be! . . .'

A contemporary of ours who had an incredibly difficult and complicated childhood received the same kindness and sympathy. She had grown up in the Shires, and at fourteen joined her parents in India. Dancing, watching polo, riding with the subalterns and revelling in the sophisticated life of the station, she lived in a state of exaltation. Then suddenly she was sent home, poured into our grey and red uniform and the atmosphere of class and common-room. She became extremely emotional. Her parents came back a little later, and there was clearly great friction between them. Long afterwards I realised that Miss Popham had extended her range to marriage counselling, albeit most discreetly! She gave the mother wonderful support, and I am almost certain that the couple continued in double harness.

Around the same time there was another girl in difficulties, which were forever landing her in disgrace. Her own school life seemed set on a rudderless course, for it ricocheted into others in a way calculated to cause explosive situations all round. Although she was tremendous fun to be with, if you weren't capsized alongside her, she was generally rated a bit of a menace! How flattering and challenging to be summoned to Miss Popham's study after lunch one day, to explore with her how best to help this girl, daughter of a distinguished sociologist, as it happened! I was only second head of my house, and torn between enjoying the colourful personality, and resenting some of the effects of it, for Aurea was an artist in undermining anyone's authority, and invariably seemed a shade larger than life. In the familiar sentiment of public-school loyalties she was 'always letting the house down'; and black stars appeared regularly against her name on our notice-board ensuring that

Dorchester House, at least, was not in the running for the
Shield of Honour! Miss Popham, as usual, treated me like an
equal and, as she puffed at her cigarette, invited suggestions.
She put it across that the child needed understanding more than
criticism, made a few shrewd observations about her health and
temperament, and explained how these interrelated, and then
described her tremendous potentialities and so on. This was a
new slant on Aurea!

Understanding: that was a trait those in any position of
responsibility were expected to develop early. The 'Parlour'—
the school name for the ruling body of prefects—chosen
primarily for qualities of leadership and integrity, was composed of heads of Houses, captains of games and a few other
seniors. All members were encouraged by Miss Popham to take
a mature view of people and events at a time when girls were
frequently treated as irresponsible children, and tended to adopt
sophisticated shallow attitudes towards their juniors. One head
of house was heard exclaiming virtuously: 'I simply can't understand you!' Later Pop made it very clear that this wasn't very
clever of her, and she was expected to try! Certain brands of
naughtiness, too, were regarded as plain stupid, and not even
meriting punishment, which tended to decrease their prestige
value.

A genuine *faux pas* didn't always evoke a cool rejoinder, for
Miss Popham had a keen sense of humour, and a sensitivity
which often saved others from embarrassment. Mrs. Woosnam-
Mills remembers how, as Olga Macdonald, she with a large
group of other Old Girls was invited down to Westonbirt for a
weekend during Pop's first term. She says, 'I walked into Mrs.
Craufurd's drawing-room and noticed several unfamiliar faces,
presumably staff. While I was talking to Mademoiselle a
pleasant new face joined us and asked my name. I stupidly
stated that the object of my visit was to see the extraordinary
person who had taken Mrs. Craufurd's place. Her eyes began
to twinkle and then she started to laugh and said that she could
quite understand my curiosity . . . I had learnt a valuable lesson

and at the same time realised that the new headmistress was not
quite as strange as I'd thought, even if she did take her two dogs
to church! Many years later I met Miss Kidney again on a
traffic island in Knightsbridge, and how delightful it was,
through her, to see Miss Popham again. . . .'

The same sentiment often prompted us to brave Pop in her
den whilst we were still very much at school. We knew that,
although she stood no higher than many a girl in Lower VI,
every inch counted, for hers was an awesome presence. Yet
along the red-carpeted corridor we came, and Mrs. West, then
Rosemary Hamilton, carries on from there:

> 'Leaning against the wall outside Miss Popham's study,
> one's hands trembled and one's inside churned in apprehen-
> sive protest. This is normal for any schoolchild waiting out-
> side the Head's study for a wigging, but a group of us often
> bore it voluntarily, for the sake of an hour's informal talk
> with Pop. In the evening, when we were left to our own
> devices, someone would say, "Let's go and talk to Pop," and
> two or three would endure the frissons of the wait in the
> passage until she was free to welcome us in. I never remember
> being turned away. As she opened the door, she gave us her
> brilliant smile, accompanied by the characteristic momentary
> widening of the eyes, which gave the impression of an inter-
> ested and vitally alert personality, which, of course, she is.
> Grouping ourselves round the fireplace on the sofa and floor,
> talk flowed uninhibited.
>
> 'Sometimes, there was a special problem. Once, we asked
> her how we could come to terms with a particular girl whom
> we all liked, but could not endure near us because of her
> breath. Whatever the problem, and however trivial, it was
> discussed fully and frankly and the talk soon went on from
> there to cover a multitude of subjects, usually including sex
> and religion. A headmistress is probably not every teenage
> girl's idea of the best authority on sex, but Pop was entirely
> feminine, very attractive and beautifully dressed. One

accepted her views on the delights and responsibilities of being a woman as from an expert. She was a passionate Christian, and, although in class she never succeeded in arousing in me more than a bored acceptance of the Old Testament as a means of passing the Scripture exam, in her life and talk she helped one immeasurably towards a firm faith.

'Ultimately, I suppose Pop, in her catalytic conversation, gave one a personality, and the means to live with it. At the time when I was at Westonbirt, "character" was all important. Looks, breeding, wealth mattered nothing, as long as you had "character". At fifteen, or thereabouts, I felt I had no particular character of my own. What do I like? Whom do I like? What am I like? I did not know the answers, but Pop was able, in those evening chats, to draw out and show one's faults and qualities, and potentialities, and give one an inkling of what might be done with them. That, surely, is education. The syllabus matters infinitely less.'

It certainly did one morning for Form IV2, when Miss Popham arrived for the usual Scripture lesson. Instead of learning the Story of Creation as narrated in Genesis, the class listened to some facts about its own creation as related by Pop! This was intriguing indeed, but difficult to relay outside. Not only had these scholars plenty else on their twelve-year-old minds, but they had not yet learnt to convey the accurate statements of facts which would later be required of them! Nevertheless, they emerged beaming, told us that *they* would nearly all become mothers, although not just yet, because Miss Popham had said so! Not a single other career had been mentioned. We devoutly hoped our turn to hear about our vocations as wives and mothers would follow on, but I don't believe it ever did! Instructions in other aspects of personal relationships was not lacking, for Pop considered that some insight into behaviour *via* elementary psychology was useful, although no substitute for exploring people's ways and needs at first hand.

Moreover, she was always ready to discuss facets of existence from a variety of standpoints. Muriel Corby says, 'I do remember her talks to us during our preparation for Confirmation, because for the first time, I was made to think about Life, and enjoyed it, although puzzled and a little daunted by the contemplation of so vast and mysterious a subject. I do, however, recall her saying once that every human life has a purpose—even though this may not be apparent to each one of us. She averred that even a child born dead may have served some purpose to its mother or father or both. This seemed to *me* to make sense and still does.'

In corresponding with school friends of the past certain qualities which Miss Popham had in great measure are underlined time and again. However she may have handled those exasperating Israelite Kings, her interpretation of other characters, whether they belonged to the Gospels, literature, the current international scene or to Westonbirt School, brought them alive, and gave them, as Rosemary Hamilton discovered, an identity. In those who sought her out, Pop frequently evoked reactions which no one, least of all themselves, previously expected. Jane Coffin, now Mrs. Evans, expounds on this theme:

'She (Miss Popham) never seemed to me in the least like a schoolmistress. She was first of all a human being who treated me as a fellow human being even when delivering a telling-off, which she was able to do most effectively.

'She had great charm which was most noticeable in her handling of my father. He would arrange to see her, to complain about some aspect of the School which he considered outrageous or undesirable, and to "lay down the law" as to what was to be altered. Invariably he emerged from the interview unusually mellowed and smiling, and saying what a perfectly delightful and intelligent woman she was. The complaint was never mentioned again.

'To many girls, myself amongst them, she was always

217

available as a counsellor, if advice were sought, or as a conversational *vis-à-vis*, ever ready to listen and exchange views, surely a rare attribute in a headmistress.

'I remember too how the whole tempo of life at Westonbirt began to quicken after her arrival. Her departure for Cheltenham after only five years at the helm of Westonbirt was a serious personal blow, as well as a very great loss for the School, which certainly needed continuity of leadership in its still young life. A certain sparkle and panache went with her. Because she has such a strong personality and been so clearcut in her likes and dislikes, of course, she has aroused opposition and controversy at times. But looking back across many years to my necessarily inexperienced judgments, Westonbirt was a much diminished place after her departure, and certainly a great deal less fun.'

This, of course, was what the School feared for itself at the end of Mrs. Craufurd's reign, and again when Miss Grubb, who brought it valiantly through the war-time years, and well out on to the other side, departed. Yet a wilting Westonbirt is yet to be seen.

The last commentary on Pop's Westonbirt phase must come from Miss Joan Badock, Head of the History Department of that day. Writing in the *Westonbirt Magazine* of November 1936, she pays this tribute to one whose sojourn amongst her staff left indelible imprints on those adult lives as well. Miss Badock and her great friend, Miss McErval, were destined to run Gardenhurst School in Somerset a year or two later:

MISS POPHAM

FIVE YEARS—not a long period in the life of any school, yet long enough in the annals of a school like Westonbirt which can, as yet, only boast its nine summers. Yet life, apart from mere existence, is not measured by time and we, who have been fortunate to work during these years under Miss Popham's leadership, have known a period made vivid by variety and contact with new ideas, sometimes bewildering but undoubtedly stimulating.

Miss Popham came to Westonbirt in 1932. For boarding schools this was perhaps the most difficult of all the post-war years. Incomes were dwindling, in some cases disappearing altogether, so that throughout the country many girls were of necessity being withdrawn from school. At such a time policy seemed to indicate a lessening of commitments, but like Marshal Foch in parallel circumstances, Miss Popham's instinct was for action. He had said in 1914, 'My right is in retreat, my centre is yielding. Situation excellent. I shall attack.' Secure in her belief in Westonbirt's future, Miss Popham's answer to such a challenge was similar. In January 1933 one of the houses in the grounds was converted for the special teaching of domestic science, while in September the first house for the training in citizenship was opened as an adjunct to the school. Within a few months the experiment had justified itself and Citizen House has been full almost since the opening day, while there are sometimes anxious moments in the school itself to discover if there really is a bed for a new girl who has been accepted.

To dwell on outward achievement is to give only one side of an intensely human personality. Which of us is not grateful for the sympathy which made Miss Popham ready at any hour of the day—and almost one might say of the night too!—to listen to the woes, however small, of staff or girls? She had no 'closing time' and few were the staff, who rising early to secure her undivided attention, did not find her already at work before them. Nothing could be more characteristic of Miss Popham than her dislike of any delay in hearing of trouble and her prompt action in dealing with its source. How often have we not heard the familiar phrase, 'Something drastic must be done', and within the hour the whole matter would have been thoroughly investigated and a permanent solution frequently found?

Dealing sympathetically with troubles of every kind is perhaps the most persistent part of a headmistress's work, yet other scenes rise before me, equally typical—Miss Popham leaping from her car to overwhelm with her anger a driver ill-treating his horse—Miss Popham putting on the dress in which she had recently been presented at Court for the benefit of those of us who had not seen it, taking trouble that it should be complete to the last bracelet, and going through the whole ceremony with great grace and seriousness before a hastily improvised sovereign and his consort complete with paper crowns—Miss Popham refusing to stop when 'gonged' for exceeding the speed limit and when asked why, replying that 'she wasn't going to let that hooting car overtake her'!

Many of us I think would agree that her most permanent gift to us all was a larger way of looking at life. Hers it was to create an atmosphere in which small jealousies found it hard to live and conventions which often seemed important in school life assumed their true proportion. Yet perhaps we shall miss most that joyous sense of life as an adventure full of unexpected demands and opportunities, to be seized wholeheartedly, unhampered by sentimental regrets. This was peculiarly hers and she expressed it for us in a prayer she often read to the school, 'Lord, we do not ask that thou wilt keep us safe but keep us ever loyal to the example of our Lord'.

APPRECIATIONS FROM CHELTENHAM

(a) The Principal's Retirement: Appreciations from the Centenary Number of the Cheltenham Ladies' College Magazine, 1953.

(b) Formal Farewell to Miss Popham by the Right Hon. Earl of Bessborough, P.C., G.C.M.G., Chairman of the Council of Cheltenham Ladies' College, July 1953.

(c) Miss W. M. Coley's Appreciation: August 1967.

(a) THE PRINCIPAL'S RETIREMENT

(It has been a most difficult task to confine within reasonable limits our appreciation of all that Miss Popham has meant to us during the sixteen years of her Principalship. We wanted to make it a truly representative expression of feeling and therefore both staff and girls were invited to contribute. Senior prefects were an obvious choice for the girls, and one who had been a housemistress for more than half Miss Popham's Principalship was finally asked to represent the staff.—Sub-Editor of Magazine)

MY FIRST meeting with Miss Popham left a deep impression on me and in later years I came to realise how characteristic that meeting had been. She wrote to me, and although it was a business letter it was full of personality and warmth. I went to visit her and found her as unusual as her letter. She was, as she always is, perfectly dressed; there was a graciousness and elegance about her and her room, and such kindness in her reception of a stranger! Perhaps the most lively impression I carried away with me was of her brilliant smile and her remarkable eyes.

When I came to work under her I found her one of those rare women, able to collect round her a group of most diverse people, all of strong personality, and from them make a team united in their devotion to the school. Miss Popham is a woman of immense vitality, unsparing of herself, a prodigious worker with a great grasp of detail, to whom no point is ever too small or unimportant for her personal attention. She always expected of her Staff the same loyalty and devotion to the College which she herself gave, and where she found such people they had her confidence and support.

Perhaps Miss Popham's greatest genius is for dealing with individuals, for she is genuinely interested in others and their problems. Once her pupil, her colleague or her friend, and her help and advice are for ever at your service. I have often known her spend much time and effort to help someone who has long since passed from her immediate circle. Probably when we think of Miss Popham the characteristic that will jump to mind is her great love of animals, and particularly of dogs. I often think that her patience with the unsuccessful, and her wise and unfailing help through the years to those who never quite find their niche, is linked in some way with her affection for lame dogs, human as well as canine.

I doubt if anyone else could have carried College through the war years with gain instead of loss when a reckoning was made at the end, for despite all the changes and makeshifts of those years College came out of them with an enhanced reputation for scholarship and education in its finest sense. Only those of us who were with her can know how the Principal had to fight and struggle to keep the College together and to get back the buildings as soon as possible. Almost anyone else would have been defeated by the difficulties, but Miss Popham is lion-hearted and, because she does not understand defeat, cannot be defeated.

To her, College was a sacred charge; she has a great reverence for scholarship and she has always felt that in a world of changing values College, with its fine standards and its tradition of putting first things first, is an important and vital influence in girls' education. To this end she held it together at all costs during the war years, and because I too believe that College stands for what is finest in English education, I recognise our incalculable debt to Miss Popham for her part in its preservation and development.

A. M. TRUESDALE
(Staff 1937–39 and Housemistress 1937–47)

MY LAST YEAR at College, soon after Miss Popham's appointment, was one of the happiest that I can remember. I have a very dear memory of Miss Popham addressing College at some early public function, probably the first Opening Prayers, and telling the story of a little dog. The dog came face to face with an advancing horde and wondered: 'If I wag, will they wag back?' I hope we did! College, with its parents and visitors, must seem a very formidable gathering, so disciplined and so silent; but Miss Popham's quiet dignity gained our instant respect. No wrong-doer could fail to tremble when called to answer for her failings, yet her friendliness made her easily accessible at all times to those needing advice and help.

Prefects, especially senior prefects, must be very difficult people to deal with; full of self-important plans, yet with no experience of power. But Miss Popham dealt with us firmly, tactfully and kindly. She had frequent meetings with us at which we could discuss problems freely and frankly. She allowed us to try our bright ideas—undoubtedly taking steps to minimise the awkward results! Consequently, our interest in the running of College was tremendously increased. I know that I made many mistakes, the results of which she quietly put right, protected me from well-deserved consequences and encouraged me to try again. What a help that was!

It was a difficult time, due to the prospect of war coming steadily nearer and, although a girls' boarding school is an excellent place in which to bury one's head in the sand, we were all infected with the universal restlessness. Miss Popham helped to relieve the tension by encouraging us to indulge in activities such as Guides and dancing, and other things connected with functions outside College. Such diversions, together with the changes in the uniform (causing it more nearly to resemble normal clothing!) helped us to feel less completely in a world apart.

To these general remarks I should like to add my own very warm, personal thanks to Miss Popham for the unfailing patience and friendship which made my last year at College such a happy one. She was always ready to listen and advise on all subjects, whether connected with College or not, and was in every way a very dear friend as well as headmistress.

MARY PRIESTLEY (MRS. CULLEN)
(Senior Prefect 1938–39)

As Others See Us

THE STORY OF Miss Popham's 'private war' and ultimate victory, which resulted in the swift return to C.L.C. of our traditional home, is all well known and still acclaimed. My object in writing is to stress one aspect of that victory—its effect upon those of us who were in College at the time and who benefited directly by her successful generalship.

For us her victory was a protection against the ill-effects of the real war, which were felt by so many of our contemporaries under less able leadership. Where they were uprooted and evacuated, our education remained stable and undisturbed. Where they may have been caught up in the national state of insecurity, we were able to retain a sense of security and calm through her example.

It would have been so easy at that time to have let high standards fall and find excuses for it; but Miss Popham had other views. Her example—in what she did and said, and how she looked—gave us the lead of calm and rational confidence, stability and morale which not only inspired us to give of our best to our work and to College, but later gave us assurance to face war-time responsibilities and conditions which might otherwise have unnerved me.

Now that she is handing over the heavy responsibilities of her office, made many times more onerous by the conditions of war and unsettled peace, we trust that her gifts of energy and courage, so unstintingly dedicated to the service of College, will enable her to enjoy her retirement to the full.

LESLEY STUART TAYLOR
(Senior Prefect 1940–41)

WITH THE COMING of peace Miss Popham's wonderful creative energy and ability were set free once more to embark upon a wider programme. Perhaps the most universally recognised of her achievements was the development of the University Entrance Department. The success of this project is undoubted, and success was achieved not least because of the high standards and infectious enthusiasm of the Principal.

But in spite of her delight in academic distinction, Miss Popham did not allow blue stockings, nor could an academic disorder of dress flourish in her presence. Her own chic, which surprised so many visitors to the 1952 Royal Academy Exhibition and exploded for all time the myth of the dowdy schoolmarm, was an inspiration to the dress-conscious and an example to the slovenly.

Wide-minded and vitally interested herself, Miss Popham felt the importance of an education in good citizenship and a wide variety of outside interests. A strong sense of relationship with the Commonwealth as a whole was fostered in College, not only by the presence of representatives of overseas countries, but also by the Principal's own connection with Canada. She brought about a happy exchange of visits between Havergal and Cheltenham. Convinced that a firm religious faith was the basis of good citizenship, Miss Popham was active in the encouragement of the teaching and practising of a practical Christianity throughout College.

It is the duty of people in high places to be interested in everything and everybody. Miss Popham more than discharged this duty. Her amazing memory for individuals enabled her to greet the smallest and shyest by name on one of her lightning trips down the Marble Corridor. Awful interviews were soon turned into informal chats by the Principal's gay humour and friendly interest—not to mention the presence of Peter. She commanded respect for herself and for her devoted and unsparing work for College, and in those of us who realised what anxieties and even weariness must often lie behind the serene cheerfulness with which she greeted College, she roused the greatest admiration. Generous with praise where praise was due and showing complete confidence in everyone she chose to help her, she had firm supporters in all those who worked closely with her because they felt she valued them.

Admiration and affection have made us proud of the Honour

which Her Majesty has bestowed on Miss Popham, and we are eager to share in the joy which such a recognition must bring.

MARIGOLD PAKENHAM-WALSH
(Senior Prefect 1948–49)

THOSE OF US who have known Miss Popham well will always remember best her truly deep religious faith. She put 'first things first' herself, and inspired in others a similar realisation of the need for spiritual values; we knew the sincerity of her own beliefs, and therefore we sought and respected her wise counsel.

The quality we all loved most in her was her gay sense of proportion. A sense of humour seems to me to be one of the first essentials of a headmistress, and Miss Popham's was superb. It was typical of her that she tested the broadcasting system for the Centenary Weekend with an Agatha Christie!

She saw problems in their right perspective and solved them with sympathy and common sense. It was a great privilege to be her senior prefect; her loyalty was absolute, her calmness and humility were an invaluable example.

JANET ROSEVEARE
(Senior Prefect 1952–53)

I CANNOT REFRAIN from adding my tribute to one whom I, like Mary, have found a real friend as well as an inspiring leader. Having been on the staff for the whole of Miss Popham's time here, I have experienced her leadership through all the four stages of which the senior prefects speak.

She has never spared herself; her amazing store of vitality has been poured out unceasingly in the service of College. Always available to parents, staff or girls, her life might have been just an unending series of interviews, yet how much else she managed to get into each crowded day! Every detail of House and College life passed through her hands and nothing of any significance ever occurred that she did not immediately know about and

228

deal with effectively and speedily. She has in full measure that rare gift in a woman of going straight to the root of a problem, tossing aside the unessential details. But her influence has not been confined to College; countless Old Girls have cause to know how her continued interest reaches out to help them in their subsequent careers, and parents also have often sought and obtained her advice and help in their personal problems.

We have delighted in her gay courage and sense of humour, her swift mind and boundless energy, her vivid personality and flair for dress; but we owe most to her for the inspiration that she has given us through her vital Christian faith, especially as it quickened us day by day in her taking of College Prayers.

V. M. HOUNSFIELD
(Sub-Editor)

(b) FORMAL FAREWELL TO MISS POPHAM

by

The Rt. Hon. the Earl of Bessborough, P.C., G.C.M.G., Chairman of the Council

Now, MISS POPHAM, what can I say to thank you for all you have done for College in the sixteen years during which you have raised the scholastic standard above that of every other girls' Public School. Your complete devotion to College, your unique personal knowledge of all the girls under your care—and of their parents—has attracted unbounded admiration from many sides. Your understanding, too, of the modern girl and, in another direction, your great respect for scholarship; these things are worthy of special words of praise. Then, too, your concern for order and discipline; it has made, as we all appreciate, a very important contribution in this casual age. The recent report on College, referred to by Miss Horsbrugh, is indeed a tribute to the work done here during your reign, work which makes College quite outstanding. But you have not only played a great part in preserving and adding to the prestige of College at home; you have also added to its repute overseas, and the number of girls coming here from all parts of the world has greatly increased under your leadership.

I believe that from the days of your early childhood you have been inspired by the desire to teach. When you came to us you had gained invaluable experience both in Canada and as head-mistress of Jersey Ladies' College and Westonbirt; in fact you had been here only a year when you made your mark, at the time when I had the honour of joining the governing body as Chairman of the Council. From that time you and I have worked together in what has been, to me, a most interesting and a most agreeable association.

Appreciations from Cheltenham

When Miss Popham and I came together about fifteen years ago, I do not think that either of us had much idea of the many worries and troubles that were before us. At the end of 1938, when the war was still a few months off, official notice arrived to say that, on the outbreak of war, the entire College buildings would be requisitioned and reserved for occupation by the War Office which would be installed in here as London was to be evacuated.

This information was conveyed under such terms of secrecy that we were not even permitted to tell the members of the governing body. What happened when war actually did break out Miss Horsbrugh has already recalled to us. Miss Popham was sustained by an unalterable determination that the College must be kept in Cheltenham. It is difficult to realise what happened in those horrid days. Houses were acquired in various directions and somehow or other—I do not still quite know how —term began miraculously in good order on the appointed day. So resolute was Miss Popham that, after a joint visit that she and I paid to the Minister of Works in London, he actually came down here and spent a day with us, which wound up by his giving instructions which made the position far less difficult. By the end of that year we had snatched back the College buildings which had stood empty awaiting Government occupation.

The next problem we had to deal with was to get the boarding houses back. This urgent need was distinctly expressed in verse in the College magazine.

> 'Miss Popham asked
> The Chairman,
> The Chairman asked
> The Government:
> "Could we have the Ladies' College
> Boarding houses back?" '*

This, in obedience to that inspired voice, was achieved almost entirely in 1941. Even in that distressful year 1940, we

* C.L.C. Magazine, Summer 1941, p. 9

231

were sufficiently organised, I remember, to receive here Her late beloved Majesty, Queen Mary, who paid us a most memorable visit. I have recounted these matters in detail because it is in dealing with the problems involved that we saw the stuff of which our Principal was made—high courage, invincible determination, amazing adaptability, driving energy, infinite resource and the exercise of much initiative. Behind all these qualities was, and remains, a deep religious conviction. As Miss Clarke says in her very able history of the College, to which Miss Horsbrugh has referred and which I also recommend most warmly to your notice: 'The Principal who took office in 1937 had to carry the College safely through a second great war: she had also to prepare its members, individually, to do battle for ideals and beliefs which could no longer be taken for granted.' That is well said.

Ever since the end of the war, with its special problems, there have been sufficient difficulties and anxieties to call for the fullest use of Miss Popham's talents and capacity. As long as I am Chairman I shall miss all the letters from the Principal, describing to me the latest situation to be dealt with and generally winding up by suggesting the solution. I have sometimes wondered whether Miss Popham has followed my advice or whether I have followed hers; I think that Miss Horsbrugh knows the answer! I can safely say that when she once pursues a particular course with determination she generally gets her way.

In the House of Lords we are said to be masters of understatement; what I have said is, at any rate, no overstatement. A very happy association now draws to an end, as it does for all of us who have been associated with Miss Popham in one way or another during her most difficult reign, and so we thank her from our hearts for all she has done and managed for Cheltenham Ladies' College and we wish her well in whatever form of service she undertakes during the many, many years of useful service that we all hope lie before her.

(c) MISS W. M. COLEY'S APPRECIATION

I WONDER whether anyone has been able to give an adequate picture of the enormously dynamic force with which Miss Popham reacted to the seemingly crushing blows dealt to C.L.C. in the autumn of 1939, and indeed, to the—again seemingly—unsurmountable obstacles of the next six years. Her whole attitude so militant and aggressive: she never 'accepted' the status quo as something to be lived with and throughout those years this petite and essentially feminine woman fought for C.L.C. as a tigress fights for her cubs. No: that is a bad comparison because there was always in her fighting something akin to the adventurous attitude of knights of old—head up and eyes ablaze but a smile lurking behind them and laughter not too far away.

I often think of those days. Recalled from holiday by telegram, travelling through the night, we, the senior members of staff, met in her drawing-room just a week before war was declared. Her vivid description of the opening of the envelopes —Secret, Very Secret, Very Very Secret—in which was revealed the name of the 'alternative accommodation' offered by the Government is still fresh in my memory. The name of it— Lilleshall Hall—meant nothing to any of us. We all took it for granted that all would be well and that, in due course we should move there lock, stock and barrel. Sworn to secrecy, in gruelling heat and shut windows (lest such activity in holiday time should betray us and spread alarm and despondency in the town) we 'marked' all furniture so that it could be neatly moved from Room 3 at C.L.C. to Room 3 at Lilleshall!

233

As Others See Us

I don't remember exactly which day it was that we met again. Miss Popham had been allowed to visit Lilleshall and she began with the news. 'I don't know whether to laugh or to cry—at the *MOST* it could only take 200.' What she *didn't* say was, 'Whatever shall we do?' We all caught the infection of her cheerful determination to do *something*. No one felt any doubts—somehow, something would be done. Miss Popham's head was up and she was not going to be beaten. She had 750 girls arriving in three weeks' time with no houses to sleep and eat in and no classrooms to be taught in, and 200 more far away in a rat-infested, beer-smelling hall (in the event 200 was hopelessly over-optimistic).

The ensuing story of the fantastic twenty days between the declaration of war and the opening-on-time of the autumn term has I hope been told by Miss Popham herself. But we who could see only a little of what this meant knew something of the vitality and resilience with which she settled down to run a school of 800 girls in two parts quite eighty miles apart! And her interest and concern for Lilleshall was no academic one. Weekend after weekend would find her driving furiously from Cheltenham to Lilleshall and back. Often some member of staff would accompany her, and would return shaken and somewhat greyer for the experience but Miss Popham would merely say gaily, 'A splendid run—cut another five minutes off my time!' Mercifully this did not go on for long but it was very high-powered while it lasted!

Other glimpses of Miss Popham I have too—battling with ministry officials and lobbying the 'top people' at the House of Commons, refusing to be dismissed from audiences with 'High-ups' till she had gained her point—likened, I believe, by one exhausted minister (or secretary?) to the importunate widow. I hope she has told that story herself.

W. M. COLEY, July 1967